# Future Law Firm Business Models

EDITED BY ALEX DAVIES

**Commissioning editor**
Alex Davies

**Editorial assistant**
Francesca Ramadan

**Published by**
Globe Law and Business Ltd
3 Mylor Close
Horsell
Woking
Surrey GU21 4DD
United Kingdom
Tel: +44 20 3745 4770
www.globelawandbusiness.com

ISBN: 978-1-78358-358-4
A catalogue record for this book is available from the British Library

# Contents

# Executive Summary

Much has been written about the pace of change facing the legal industry – how certain law firm functions are being replaced by artificial intelligence and new types of service providers, how accounting firms are looking to absorb and replace law firms, and how merging into worldwide megafirms of 3,000 to 10,000 lawyers is the only way to survive. Steve Jobs and others have called this evolution "creative destruction". Richard Susskind referred to it years ago as "the end of lawyers".

It is true that the legal market is facing massive change. Technology, new ways of working, alternative methods of billing, and highly disruptive new entrants have all made their mark on the traditional legal business model. *Future Law Firm Business Models* takes a look at all these trends and more, horizon-scanning for future developments, and delving into the ways in which these issues will fundamentally change the market.

Beginning with the legal ecosystem, the first few chapters look at structure and skills. The book opens with an overview by Michael Roster, formerly managing partner of Morrison & Foerster's Los Angeles office, and co-chair of the firm's financial services practice group worldwide, who believes that it is inevitable that lawyers and their law firms will be (in the main) replaced by highly efficient multi-disciplinary practices (MDPs) that offer bundled services and yield measurably better outcomes at a fraction of current costs. If done right, he argues, MDPs will be far more satisfying places to work, although lawyers may find they play significantly different roles. The question for leaders at law and accounting firms, he maintains, as well as for general counsel and other corporate executives, is whether they get ahead of the curve or find that these changes eventually are thrust upon them.

In the future world of work, lawyers can no longer be *just* lawyers, regardless of whether they work in private practice or a corporate legal department. Much, much more is required. A lawyer needs to be an efficiency expert, trained in the worlds of lean and Six Sigma to drive waste out of processes designed by lawyers over the ages to be waste-filled.

A lawyer needs to be skilled in after action assessments, penetrating examinations of how problems arose, what could have prevented the mistake, the problem, the root cause of an adverse event. A lawyer needs to be a skilled change management agent, helping business operators change in ways that will improve operations and decrease demand for legal services. As corporations become more global and the scope of a general counsel's responsibilities grow faster than the law department budget, radically new demands are being imposed on general counsel. Chapter 2 by Patrick Lamb of ElevateNext explores those demands in more depth, identifying emerging solutions, and discussing the growing role of law companies, the Big Four, tech companies and others in the delivery of legal solutions.

While the Big Four are becoming newly involved in legal services in the US, this trend has already been present in the UK market for a number of years. Chapter 3 looks at how the legal market is changing in direct response to the arrival of the Big Four into the legal sector, focusing specifically on EY Law, one of the forerunners of this trend. Matthew Kellett explains how EY is expanding its legal services offering, and why he believes there is room for everybody in the market.

In chapter 4, Rachel Khiara of Khiara Law considers the practical challenges for a multi-disciplinary practice from a regulatory perspective. The chapter explores the UK's Solicitors Regulatory Authority (SRA) jurisdiction, regulatory conflicts, and the complex position of lawyers and non-lawyers delivering client services jointly as part of a team. Her chapter considers the differences between providing legal and non-legal services within an MDP, and looks at the difficult issue of legal professional privilege to the extent that it is available under the UK's Legal Services Act 2007. The chapter provides some practical advice for the MDP's compliance officers, their scope of responsibilities, working alongside other regulators and some hidden traps for client monies. By exploring the regulatory structure and impact of MDPs in the UK market, Rachel brings forward the key issues that will need addressing in any market where MDPs exist.

Moving on to the theme of clients, in chapter 5, Tony Young of BDO explores the changing nature of client relationships. Utilizing the findings from original research carried out by the firm, he explains how clients increasingly want lawyers to be more like business partners – to bring ideas to the table that can help them in their businesses, and present more creative ways to add value. The managing partners consulted for the research referred to connectivity, integration, collaboration, new ways of delivery and closer relationships/partnerships. This all points to firms considering new client relationships where being an integral part of the team and not just a service provider will be key to future success and survival. For some there is great opportunity to prosper and this is already part of the strategy for growth. Other firms predicted a move towards "strategic partnerships" and a shift away from purely transactional engagements with clients. This means lawyers and other experts within the firm will provide more advice and support to their clients outside specific matters and often outside technical legal issues, dramatically changing the business model dynamic.

In chapter 6, Chris Howe of Raedbora Consulting discusses how the pressures for new business models mean alternative fee arrangements (AFAs) are finally coming of age. Fixed fees are now quite commonplace in some markets but more radical change has been limited. However, the relentless pressure for value, new entrants to the market, and the greater leverage clients hold – not just on price but on legal quality and process – mean that law firms are building different business models to meet these needs and as a result AFAs become not just necessary, but a logical component of the new landscape. As a result, the next ten years are likely to see more change for more firms than the last 60. The successful firms will ride this wave and come to dominate the market.

Chapter 7, by Robert Millard of Cambridge Strategy Group, steers the book towards technological trends. AI, Blockchain, big data, the IoT, advanced wireless networks and perhaps even quantum computing – acting together in dynamic, complex concert – seem poised to transform commerce, industry, and society itself. If that proves to be so, the legal profession will need to remodel itself on a scale unprecedented in a century if it is to adequately serve the needs of clients and society in the new world that results.

The rise of the law company as a business in legal services has potential to be a Blue Ocean category, separate and apart from lawyer-centric and law firm partner models. This emerging category places emphasis on outputs rather than inputs – with less deference to lawyer "stars" as the main service delivery. With no legacy cultures of adoption resistance, those starting today can have continuous process improvement and investment in technology as strategic advantages along with multi-disciplinary approaches to client identified (business) challenges. The services may be merely tangentially, rather than wholly, tied to those providing legal advice. Companies such as Atrium, Elevate, and previously Clearspire are all geared toward a new offering, backed by capital and corporate structures and "full stack supply chain" rather than legal exclusive solutions. Success is not measured by profit per partner and there is potential for greater and new forms of value creation.

Atrium is a full-service corporate law firm that uses modern technology to give start-ups a legal experience that is fast, transparent, and price-predictable. Founded by Twitch founder and Y Combinator partner, Justin Kan, along with Augie Rakow, a corporate partner at a major Silicon Valley law firm, the company came into being in order to solve Justin's own problem as a founder: making legal faster and more transparent, with upfront pricing. In chapter 8, Jason Moyse, who describes himself as working at the intersection of the business of law, legal innovation and technology, discusses the rise of law companies, providing insights into the future direction of legal services from the customer's point of view.

In order to keep pace with the changing workforce demographic, law firms of the future will have to adapt their business models to suit the needs of multiple generations. Chapter 9, by Rachel Brushfield of EnergiseLegal, explores generational differences and their impact on the employer of the future, including motivations and career drivers. Incorrect myths about the millennial generation are dispelled, implications on traditional workforce management practices are shared, and practical tips and self-reflective questions are provided to begin introducing change.

The legal profession is experiencing rapid and meaningful transformation in both the practice and business of law. Disruption is being driven by new business models, technology, data and analytics, globalization and the evolution of in-house groups. In the final three chapters of the book, we look at how finance is changing the legal landscape. Litigation finance is enabling law firms and clients to leverage capital to overcome obstacles to gaining access to justice, reallocate expenses reserved for legal fees on their P&Ls to investments in their products and employees, and to drive expansion and growth. Law firms are also leveraging litigation finance to better differentiate themselves, while in-house clients use it to position themselves as strategic assets rather than solely as service groups. Chapter 10, by Scott Mozarsky of Vannin Capital, focuses on the challenges and opportunities that gave rise to litigation finance, as well as the impact it is having in making the legal market function in a more efficient and logical manner. It also focuses on key trends and how the litigation finance market will evolve moving forward.

In chapter 11, Jae Um of Six Parsecs reviews the changing landscape of the legal sector, discussing how access to capital is changing the way law firms operate.

Finally, in chapter 12, Rachel Khiara looks at the UK's Alternative Investment Market (AIM), and considers how the future of the UK legal services market will change as firms start to dip their toe into the public domain and a new group of "Public Circle" firms emerges alongside the Magic Circle and Silver Circle in the UK market. Should this be on the partners' agenda for every ambitious mid-tier firm? With some law firms having already floated on the London Stock Exchange, with some success, these developments will be interesting for anyone involved in managing a legal services business anywhere in the world.

# About the authors

**Rachel Brushfield** is the talent liberator at EnergiseLegal, a career strategist, coach, marketing mentor and published author with over 30 years' experience. Helping women lawyers to "blow their own trumpet" is a specialism. Rachel's career heritage is in marketing and brand strategy and communications for communication agencies including J Walter Thompson, expertise she now uses to help women lawyers to liberate their talent and market themselves confidently and competently.

Services include individual career coaching, executive coaching, events, workshops, and content creation for The Law Society, AWS, LexisNexis and AWLL. Rachel is a published author in talent management, professional development, work–life balance, gender balance, career management and marketing yourself. She is co-founder of PWHub – Inspiring Professional Women, a network exclusively for senior women employed in Oxfordshire companies – and was shortlisted in the entrepreneur category of the WeAreTheCity 2017 "Rising star" awards, one of only 200 women in the UK.

**Chris Howe** is a director of Raedbora Consulting and advises clients in legal on pricing, practice management, including restructuring and day to day performance improvement, and the operational aspects of mergers. He also advises buyers of legal services on legal procurement reviews. His clients include top 20 international law firms as well as FTSE 100 businesses. Chris was for 10 years divisional director and commercial director of a UK top 20 Law firm where he was head of pricing and conducted innovative research into pricing with Cranfield School of Management. He also has 10 years' consulting experience with PwC, Ernst & Young, and Deloitte. Chris is an international speaker and author on pricing and professional services. He holds an MA from University of Cambridge and is a chartered accountant.

**Matthew Kellett** is head of law in EY's UK Financial Services Organization. He joined in 2014 to establish the practice, and now leads teams focused on legal transformation (supporting in-house legal departments in setting strategy, managing legal risk, and transforming the function to meet the changing needs of the business), legal managed services, and financial services regulation. Prior to joining EY, Matthew was a partner at Linklaters, before going into banking. He returned to the legal profession in 2010 as head of finance at BLP. He is a frequent speaker on the changing face of the legal profession and the rise of LawTech.

**Rachel Khiara** is recognized as a leading lawyer advising law firms and new entrants into the legal services sector on all aspects of governance, management, regulation, structural and financial reform. Khiara Law provides assistance on ground-breaking deals in the legal services sector and is one of the most experienced advisors available to ABS applicants. The firm's excellence in Partnership and LLP law is recognised in both *Legal 500 UK Directory* and *Chambers & Partners* Directory.

**Patrick Lamb** is founding partner of ElevateNext Law, LLP, and vice president of Elevate Services, Inc. Pat and his long-time partner Nicole Auerbach founded ElevateNext Law in 2018 to provide legal services in alignment with Elevate Services, a global law company. The unique arrangement armed ElevateNext with global capabilities and a wide array of additional tools to utilize in crafting solutions for its customers. ElevateNext allows Elevate to offer its customers services that include practice of law areas it previously had to defer to other law firms. Pat has been a long-time innovator in the delivery of legal services. Having launched Valorem Law Group in January 2008, Pat became the leading voice for alternative fee structures in all types of legal matters, including complex business litigation. Valorem has been recognized by clients and others as one of the leading AFA firms in the country. Pat pioneered the essential relationship between alternative fees and client service, and has long argued that alternative fees are but one of several essential tools that should be deployed to serve clients. Pat has been recognized four times as a BTI Consulting Client Service All-Star MVP, and Valorem has been named six times a member of the BTI Client Service A-Team.

Pat remains an active practicing lawyer but now is devoting considerable attention to designing solutions for customer issues that help avoid litigation and disputes. He has tried numerous cases around the country and draws on his long experience as a litigator and trial lawyer to design effective solutions. He is in great demand as a speaker, at both public and private events. He is a prolific writer, including his periodic column for the *ABA Journal's* award-winning New Normal section and his blog, *In Search of Perfect Client Service*, www.patrickjlamb.com. His latest book, *Alternative Fee Arrangements for Litigators and their Clients*, was published by the ABA in 2014. He can be found on Twitter at @ElevateLamb.

**Robert Millard** is director of Cambridge Strategy Group (CSG,) a virtual management consultancy in the UK that utilizes a sophisticated digital collaboration platform to leverage a network of leading specialists in a variety of areas of business strategy and management. The firm is focused primarily on professional services and other deep knowledge enterprises. Rob is immediate past co-chair of the IBA's Law Firm Management Committee and currently serves on the steering committee of the IBA's "President's task force on the future of legal services". He is based in Cambridge, UK, but his clients span the globe.

**Jason Moyse** has served on global teams implementing major customer experience initiatives as a connector/doer/spark and key trusted advisor to the c-suite, senior leadership and governance teams for legal and business matters. His broad background includes private legal practice in high volume commercial litigation as well as serving as in-house counsel in legal and business roles. A member of various boards centered on legal innovation including MDR Labs, he is also the principal of Law Made – an agency supporting the makers of legal innovation. Previously, he co-created and executed on the vision of LegalX through the MaRS Discovery District. Jason also serves as manager of legal business solutions on behalf of Elevate Services – a next-generation legal service provider helping law firms and corporate legal departments improve efficiency, quality, and outcomes through consulting, managed services, technology, and talent.

**Scott Mozarsky** is Vannin Capital's managing director – North America, with overall responsibility for Vannin's North American business. Prior to joining Vannin, Scott was president of Bloomberg Law, leading Bloomberg's business across the legal market. Scott was also responsible for building and leading the Bloomberg Next organization across Bloomberg's industry verticals, which included Bloomberg BNA, Bloomberg Government and Bloomberg New Energy Finance. Prior to joining Bloomberg, Scott held a number of executive business and legal roles during a 13-year tenure in the United Business Media plc Group. As president – media and marketing services for UBM Tech, he was responsible for building UBM Tech's marketing services business and driving the evolution of leading websites such as Information Week.com and EE Times. As EVP chief commercial officer of its subsidiary, PR Newswire, Scott oversaw PRN's commercial activities worldwide, which involved spearheading the company's efforts to meet the communications, marketing, investor relations and compliance needs of its customers. From 2002-09, Scott served as general counsel and headed up global corporate development and M&A for United Business Media Limited's US-based subsidiaries. In that role, his organization played a lead role in transforming UBM from a North American-centric print media group to a global provider of integrated digital and live event solutions. Scott also spent eight years at two multinational law firms representing media, technology, telecommunications, insurance and manufacturing companies. Scott, who speaks Japanese and lived in Japan, has advised numerous companies on business, financial and legal issues arising out of cross-border transactions.

**Michael Roster** was formerly managing partner of Morrison & Foerster's Los Angeles office, co-chair of the firm's Financial Services Practice Group worldwide, and a member of the firm's policy committee. In 1993, Mike was appointed general counsel of Stanford University, Stanford Medical Center, and Stanford Management Company. He was subsequently executive vice president and general counsel of Golden West Financial Corporation. Mike has also served as chair of the Association of Corporate Counsel, as outside director and vice chair of Silicon Valley Bank, chair of the Stanford Alumni Association, steering committee co-chair of ACC's Value Challenge, and chair of two start-up companies. He currently teaches Contract Drafting and Analysis at the University of Southern California Gould School of Law and is a director of MDRC in New York, a nonprofit organization that evaluates the effectiveness of government and other programs affecting lower- and moderate-income families and individuals.

**Jae Um** is an insights analyst and business designer for fast-changing legal markets, with more than ten years of legal industry experience. Jae leverages diverse skills across design-driven research, visual analytics, strategy development, and creative storytelling to generate insights that busy, important people actually want to read and are able to use. She is a contributing author to *Legal Evolution, American Lawyer*, and other publications covering the legal industry. Prior to Six Parsecs, Jae served in a progression of high-impact roles in client service innovation and strategic growth at Seyfarth Shaw.

As a partner in BDO Brisbane's Business Services division, **Tony Young** provides taxation and commercial advice to a diverse selection of clients, including professionals, property developers, manufacturers and retailers. Tony works with clients from a wide range of backgrounds, particularly family owned and operated businesses and professional service firms looking to grow their operations.

As lead partner of the firm's estate planning service offering, Tony works proactively with his clients to protect their assets and eliminate confusion surrounding their financial affairs. He works in conjunction with his clients, their solicitor and financial planner to deliver a comprehensive estate plan that meets their unique needs. Major achievements to date include planning and implementing the succession strategy for a substantial family owned enterprise, which involved solving significant tax and stamp duty problems and working within the family dynamics to ensure a cohesive management group. Tony has also been involved in significant restructures of professional service firms, including incorporations, mergers and acquisitions.

# Chapter 1: The inevitability of multi-disciplinary practices

*By Michael Roster, formerly managing partner of Morrison & Foerster's Los Angeles office*

Much has been written about how lawyers are being replaced by artificial intelligence and new types of service providers, accounting firms are absorbing and replacing law firms, and mergers into worldwide megafirms of 3,000 to 10,000 lawyers is the only way to survive. Steve Jobs and others have called the process "creative destruction". Richard Susskind referred to it years ago as the end of lawyers.

I believe these are merely symptoms and, in most cases, wrong responses to what is happening: *the disaggregation of what lawyers traditionally have done*. Over time, in my view and with some exceptions, lawyers and their law firms will be replaced with highly efficient multi-disciplinary practices (MDPs) that offer bundled services and yield measurably better outcomes at a fraction of current costs.

If done right, MDPs will also be far more satisfying places to work, although lawyers may find they play significantly diminished roles, whether as outside or in-house counsel. As part of the transformation, the chief legal officer/general counsel will often be replaced by a newly created position of chief risk/compliance/solutions officer, who sometimes will be a lawyer, sometimes not.

In my opinion, the accounting firms won't be the right platform. They are too big, rigid and, given their audit culture, process-oriented rather than outcomes-oriented. In addition, they will need to be split up still once again because of regulatory and company requirements for independent auditors.

Law firms largely won't be the winners either. Lawyers typically aren't good managers. Our training is to identify issues (the "what if" part of what we do) but only a small set of really good lawyers are also good at the other half of the equation, which is "so what". That is, lawyers who have the expertise and confidence to decide what really matters and then to advise a client what actually to do. The megafirms will be especially inefficient given their high overhead and income expectations versus the more granular pricing that is needed for diverse practice groups to be competitive.

Layered on top of all of this will be the problem of conflicts. The efficient provider of multi-disciplinary services will serve hundreds of entities in the same lines of business; those entities may have similar issues but also periodically may sue one another, as well as do deals with one another. As a former general counsel of a major university and medical center and then a nationwide financial services company, I never had a problem with a law firm representing my competitors in compliance and similar matters. I knew from my own days as a law firm partner that these firms would have greater expertise and reliability because they handle hundreds of similar matters and clients. My senior management was fine with that as well. What my fellow executives and board members couldn't accept was that a law firm with which we had shared highly sensitive information might periodically be on the other side, suing us. And what many law firm leaders don't seem to realize is, this doesn't turn simply on bar association rules of ethics. It's the appearance of it that impacts a company's senior managers.

Finally, most MDP work will be performed by highly skilled professionals who aren't lawyers. They will see no benefit in being housed in the large accounting and law firms that impose procedures that undermine efficiency and have overhead that undercuts competitive pricing.

Let me explain with two examples.

## Stanford construction

Years ago, when I was general counsel at Stanford University and Stanford Medical Center, we were doing over $1 billion in construction in a short span of years. Our architects and contractors were people and companies with whom Stanford had longstanding relationships, some for over 100 years and with whom we would continue working in the future. But problems sometimes arose as inevitably will happen with any construction, be it remodeling a kitchen or building a new hospital.

For lack of any place else, the disputes typically came to the general counsel's office. As I used to say in speeches, few if any of the issues were legal. What we needed to do was figure out where various parties had fallen short and how then to adjust the pricing. Finding those answers would most efficiently draw upon the expertise and methodologies of project managers, accountants, architects, and engineers – not the skills and methodologies of lawyers. Taking depositions and arguing in front of judges or even arbitrators are expensive alternatives and not readily adapted to solving these kinds of problems.

So I used to say, find me a multi-disciplinary team that could review our files and those of our service providers. Take two weeks, maybe a month at the most, and I'll pay the team $100,000 to tell us and the other parties how best to allocate the liabilities. Let's assume they would come back and say something like: the architect's plans were terrific but had some design flaws, so 20 percent exposure there; the general contractor did good work but failed to properly supervise some of the subcontractors, so 30 percent exposure there; and the remaining 50 percent of the costs were because of all the undocumented change orders from Stanford.

I think we all would say, fine, you've done what is needed and we then would adjust the pricing among ourselves.

But I'd then go back to this MDP team and say, here's another $100,000. Put into place a system that will better monitor and manage our construction projects going forward. Use best practices you've learned from similar matters and companies. And then I'd go one step further. Here's another $10,000 to $25,000. Every six months, come and audit the systems you put in place. Are we following them or are we starting to make costly mistakes again? And if our construction managers are finding some better approaches, incorporate them into your systems for us and even for your other clients.

Given our total construction costs, this alternative MDP approach would be a fraction of what traditional dispute resolution entails for Stanford and entities like us. Plus, since donors often helped cover our shortfalls, they used to regularly tell me that they would personally donate funds to implement these sorts of procedures.

## European food company

I was in London several years ago and had lunch with Richard Susskind, author of *The End of Lawyers?*.[1] That evening, I had dinner with a long-time friend and his wife. He owns and is CEO of a major food processor in Europe. I told him about my lunch with Susskind and also about the Association of Corporate Counsel's "Value Challenge"[2] and asked what his company was doing about its own legal costs.

"Oh, lawyers," he replied. "We don't use them anymore." He then told me about a UK company that provides a comprehensive service at a fixed price for HR and health and safety, the two areas that used to account for 95 percent or more of his legal costs. This entity largely doesn't advise his managers but instead performs the functions directly. That is, they write his company's employment and health and safety manuals; they update the manuals as they see trends among their many other clients and their interactions with regulators; they train his senior people as well as the workforce; and they regularly audit for compliance.

And then my friend noted, almost in passing, "Oh yeah, and if we get sued, which almost never happens anymore, they have some lawyers who handle it". This result is very similar to what we achieved at Stanford with our major outsourcing/partnering years ago. When expertise is properly brought to bear, the number of disputes falls dramatically – at Stanford, after five years of the partnering/outsourcing, we had half the litigation as we had had the prior decade, even while our legal costs had been reduced by 25 percent.

My friend in the UK loved the fact that what once was a major uncertainty in his annual budget – the costs of compliance and disputes – was now a fixed line item. It also was a huge benefit that the few disputes that now arose internally or with his regulators were quickly resolved and that he and his management team could instead focus on running the company.

If you think about it, what this MDP is doing for my friend and numerous companies like his is what law firms and in-house corporate counsel also largely do: we are monitoring for trends and deploying our expertise. But the MDP is able to directly solve problems, something we lawyers aren't authorized to do. Put more starkly, the MDP has the authority and expertise to be proactive, not simply reactive.

## Platforms

I've already noted why law firms and accounting firms may not be the best platforms for offering MDP services.

One way they might become more workable platforms would be to give internal practice groups much greater autonomy in determining how best to staff themselves and price their services. Many practice groups would likely find they could actually increase profitability by reducing hourly rates, something that is anathema to most law firm chairs. Profitability would turn instead on a practice group increasing efficiency, as well as the number of clients served. In most cases, this also would mean pricing services at a fixed or similar approach and not by the hour. Rather, hours would be used, if at all, solely as a way to monitor internal costs of production and where the goal would be to continually reduce the cost of hourly work units as well as the number of work units needed to accomplish a task. A related goal would be for the practice group to be financially rewarded by clients for outcomes versus costs of production.

The idea that a law firm or accounting firm should be run top-down by a dominant CEO works against all of this. Rather, law firms and accounting/consulting firms are more like a hotel that provides space and basic services to its residents and otherwise stays out of their way.

Another analogy is to a university or medical center. Yes, we at Stanford or Amherst or Cleveland Medical Clinic all have a brand, and we watch for any departments that might not be maintaining the expected quality. But otherwise each academic or medical department is fairly autonomous. That is, what an English department pays a professor is quite different from what is paid to a dermatologist or heart transplant surgeon. And by the way, although the dermatologist's billing rate may be a fraction of the heart transplant surgeon's billing rate, the department of dermatology is often far more profitable than the surgery department. High billing rates do not necessarily equate with high profitability.

Subsidiaries of law or accounting firms largely won't work either because of the "heads I win, tails you lose" syndrome. If the subsidiary is barely breaking even after the parent receives its payments for overhead or profits, the subsidiary's workers likely will stay. On the other hand, if the subsidiary is highly successful, its leaders and workers eventually will want to be spun off or will leave on their own. The issue is made even more complicated since a lot of the target market will be clients of other law or accounting firms who aren't going to send work to the subsidiary of a competitor.

In reality, most MDPs will find the best platform for them is an independent entity that they own and control and is devoted solely to their and maybe one or two related practices. As a result, everyone in the entity will have a common bond of expertise. There will be much wider career opportunities throughout the organization – for example, a sales manager could someday be CEO, something usually not possible at a law or accounting firm. The technology staff will no longer be in some remote department that is stretched thin and often doesn't even understand what individual units do. Rather, technology staff members will be fully integrated with the business and will often see major ways to improve efficiency and client satisfaction. Technology staff members might even be placed on site with various clients to integrate what the MDP is doing for those clients, including where the services are being offered on a total outsourced basis.

## Privilege

Legal privilege will still be important and will be a problem for MDPs. It's why law firms that are devoted to litigation may have a very strong future. But to be competitive, they will need to learn how to quickly and efficiently match up with a specific MDP, assess the exposures, maintain privilege, draw upon the MDP's expertise and then develop a successful advocacy plan.

Something similar will be needed internally at a company. That is, if some portion of litigation is kept in-house, there will need to be sufficient separation so that privilege can be maintained. That might mean an executive vice president for risk, compliance, and solutions, to whom the general counsel/head of litigation reports, but where their interactions are carefully set up in order to preserve privilege.

## Conflicts

I've already discussed the problem of conflicts when a law firm and in some cases an accounting firm tries to be the platform for MDP services. The conflicts issue alone will be a serious impediment for law firms to deploy MDP services.

And yes, I know many firms seek blanket conflicts waivers. Most of us general counsel properly won't give such waivers but rather need to consider the issues case by case. I always bent over backwards to let my law firms represent other entities. But as I said, it isn't solely a question of the rules of ethics, it's also how this comes across to my senior managers. If I tell them this outside law firm is just like me, and truly devoted to the company so my managers can share highly sensitive information, imagine how I come across if, a few months later, those same lawyers are on the other side against us. And no, my telling my senior management that the firm (supposedly) has an ethical wall in place doesn't satisfy their concerns. For the law firm to properly maintain standards and deploy its expertise, its lawyers need to share information. So even if they don't name my company in their practice group and other internal meetings, they actually are sharing information about my company.

## Possible transition

There may be a useful way for law, accounting, and other professional services firms to transition from their current structures to what I have suggested is ahead for MDPs.

That would be to informally divide the firm's current professional groups between those that are best positioned for offering MDP services versus those that will continue to provide the current and more traditional services. For example, a group within the environmental department at a law firm might be separated into the advisory and compliance group and allowed to develop a different approach to that practice. This might include different pricing, including fixed prices; the addition of more nonlawyers, some of whom might be paralegals but many of whom might carry titles such as "compliance specialist," "advisory assistant" and the like; and over time the development of very different interactions with clients. As noted in my discussion about the European food company, these entities might often provide their services on a total outsourcing basis for many companies.

Similar approaches might be tried in labor, benefits, tax, and similar areas.

Parallel to those units would be groups that handle litigation or other types of disputes in a given substantive area, with the common feature being that privilege is very important to that group's work and that the matters they are handling are being prepared for actions pending before a court or other tribunal. Something similar would be done at the accounting firms in transition and where independence is important for a specific type of work and thus the consulting and outsourcing role is inappropriate.

The law, accounting, or other professional services firm would then monitor how these parallel groups develop, but being in the position to someday spin off the MDPs into one or more separate firms. The original firms might offer support services on contract to the spun-off MDPs, but with an understanding that management would now be entirely separate so that privilege for the legal group, independence for the audit group, etc. can be maintained.

During the period of transition, lawyers and paralegals would have time to decide which career paths make the most sense for them, and the practice groups and the firms likewise would learn during the transition period what works well and what might need to be done differently.

The end result would be something similar to what I have otherwise described. MDPs ultimately would exist in one or more separate entities that specialize in particular areas (HR, environmental, corporate compliance, etc.). What remains in the traditional law firm would largely be focused on litigation and other forms of dispute resolution. Similarly, what remains at the traditional accounting firm would be what is required for independent audits.

I believe this transition is inevitable. The question for leaders at law and accounting firms, as well as general counsel and other corporate executives, is whether they get ahead of the curve or find that these changes eventually are thrust upon them.

### *References*

1. Susskind, R. *The End of Lawyers?: Rethinking the nature of legal services*, Oxford University Press, 2008.
2. www.acc.com/valuechallenge/

Chapter 2:

# A world without lines means lawyers have to move beyond just law

*By Patrick Lamb, founding partner of ElevateNext Law, LLP and vice president, Elevate Services, Inc.*

When I started practicing law, excellent lawyers were identified by their ability to know or research "the law" and apply "the law" to facts so clients could make decisions. Lawyers of all ages spent a lot of time reading cases to understand the law and then writing briefs or memorandum to argue to judges how he or she should apply the law. White papers were popular and 50-state surveys of a legal nicety were in vogue. The practice of law was all about "the law".

Then the world began shifting. We moved from simply learning and knowing the law, to applying it for clients. This era was the heyday of two-handed lawyers, who advised clients in classic "on one hand.... and on the other..." fashion.

These changes continued. As they say, "shift happens", and we have shifted through eras at a faster and still faster rate. These new eras have included the one where excellence was knowing the business and becoming a trusted advisor, to the one where budgeting and price predictability was the critical attribute, and, to a lesser degree, to the efficiency era.

Each era was an add-on to prior areas – lawyers were evolving, but always inside the legal vertical. The pace of this change was sufficiently fast that some debate whether law is going through evolution or revolution. As if the characterization matters. Change, be it evolution or revolution, is happening at an accelerating pace. And, as with all changes, those who adapt first have the best chance of coming out a winner, while those slow to adapt have the best chance of finding their way to history's scrap heap.[1] Thus, it is important to understand the direction of change. No one can be 100 percent correct in predicting change with precision, but understanding change from a directional standpoint helps decision-makers orient their organizations in the right direction.

## Where we are now

The role of general counsel or chief legal officer is complex. According to Altman Weil's 2018 Chief Legal Officer Survey, CLOs spend 37 percent of their time advising their organizations' executives, 22 percent practicing law, 20 percent on other corporate responsibilities – *and just 18 percent of their time managing the law department.*[2] Despite the relatively little time spent managing the law department, CLOs admit there is a growing expectation from their CEOs that the law department operates like other business units in the company.

This isn't new, just more prominent than ever before. "More with less" has become a mantra for nearly all corporate law departments, and they have found many ways to serve this mantra. Since approximately 2010, law departments have been growing in size to cover an increased overall workload. Law firms were not an option for this growing work demand: law firms were – and remain – too expensive. And many law departments sought assistance in taming the law firm beast. Almost 40 percent of all law departments employ a legal operations professional, up six points in just two years.

It is apparent that even as demand grows, law departments are attempting to address this demand with an approach other than further use of outside counsel. Most law departments responded by increasing their headcount and bringing work inside that previously was handled by their law firms. We are in an era where law departments aggressively compete with their own law firms.

There is a clear, unambiguous message in such data and trends. Law firms, however, appear not to have gotten the memo. Though the US inflation rate in 2018 is less than 2 percent, billing rate growth is running at almost 4.5 percent, a return to halcyon days of more than a decade ago. Firms continue to rely on steep billing rate increases to generate profits and pay for exorbitant increases to associate salaries (now $190,000 for many new associates). General counsel know they can hire highly experienced in-house attorneys for that amount. Still, firms keep doing what they have always done.

The legal world, however, is no longer about just law firms. Since the 1990s, law companies have been carving out a piece of the legal pie, now capturing over $8 billion in legal revenue. That amount is growing at an incredible pace as more law departments learn the value that law companies and alternative legal service providers can deliver.

## Where do we go from here?

Herbert Stein, an esteemed economist and former chair of the Counsel of Economic Advisors, is the creator of Stein's Law, which applies to the legal market:

*If something cannot go on forever, it will stop.*

The current trends cannot sustain themselves, leaving only the questions of when they will stop and whether they will end through a slow and natural transition to a new era or because a cataclysmic event forces change. The experience of the Great Reset in 2008 should be fresh enough in many minds to lead people to believe change will be driven by an event rather than be something that "just happens". Bill Gates famously said, "We always overestimate the change that will occur in the next two years and underestimate the change that will occur in ten. Don't let yourself be lulled into inaction."

If we look closely, we can now see the direction of looming change. We can see enough that we know the change will likely be profound. And despite Bill Gates' viewpoint, we also know that the pace of change, particularly in the business world, is accelerating. Think in exponential terms, not geometric. And because the legal world is so linked to the business world, the pressure for law to keep up will be intense.

Let's look at several threads and consider whether they weave together:

1. Law firms continue to increase their cost structures, most recently seen in significant salary increases for their associates;
2. Law firms have not materially changed their business model, still favoring expensive downtown real estate in major cities, reducing their ability to materially reduce their cost structure;
3. Client demands are increasing as businesses become larger and more global, with so many regulatory and compliance issues;
4. Lean, Six Sigma and other process-focused disciplines have become well-entrenched in the business world, while the "we're special" claims from lawyers seeking to be exempted from such thinking have become party jokes;
5. In-house counsel are rapidly learning that fundamental components of much of their legal work are best handled in a highly structured, process-led, scalable and repeatable manner, helping

law departments fit into the Lean/Six Sigma/process-focused world of their business colleagues;

6. Chief legal officers are serving more and more as strategic business partners to fellow c-suite executives, changing their roles to essential business executives, which changes the way they look at their own law departments;
7. Technology continues to evolve in law and, more importantly, outside of law, leading CLOs and others in law departments to embrace the critical role that the right technology can play in achieving the law departments' missions;
8. Alternative Legal Service Providers (ALSPs) working in staffing have shown that labor arbitrage works, but only to a degree since it does not reduce demand for services;
9. Law companies, which take the ALSP model to the next level, have established that the delivery of managed legal services can achieve better, predictable quality at lower cost, and with tech and other features, can reduce demand on law department resources; and
10. The Big Four accounting firms have cast their eyes on legal. PwC now employs 2,500 attorneys globally. EY employs 2,100, Deloitte 2,000 and KPMG brings up the rear at 1,700.[3] To put these numbers in perspective, if these groups within the Big Four were standalone law firms, each would be one of the 30 largest firms in the world. The Big Four have yet to focus on the US market, but such focus seems only a matter of time.

Despite these threads, the most important trend may be about lines. Not ones that you wait in, but the lines on organizational charts. The legal profession has always existed in a binary world of lines that defined the legal vertical. Inside counsel versus outside counsel. Law department versus law firm. Indeed, law department versus business unit. Partner versus associate. Plaintiff's lawyer versus defense lawyer. Always one or the other, never "all of the above". These types of lines are not unique in the legal vertical, but they are more pronounced and meaningful than in any other area.

We are now learning these historic lines hinder business success. As a result, there is growing pressure to bypass, erase or otherwise overcome these lines. Some examples demonstrate this:

1. The problem: A large company selling a commodity product has several thousand contracts per month. It has a large, consistent number of disputes with its customers relating to the products being ordered. These disputes lead to compromises with the customers, resulting in erosion of profit margin in a low margin workstream. The disputes are handled by the law department and consume significant in-house time. The issue is whether legal or operations controls is responsible for fixing the problem.

   The solution: Ignore the lines. External consultants review the contracting workflow used by the business, leading to workflow revisions and automation of portions of the process. The new approach would yield process cost savings and less erosion to thin margins. It also reduces demand on the law department, freeing up its resources to address other issues.
2. The problem: Contract disputes frequently occur because the people who are supposed to perform the contract were not the ones who negotiated it, do not understand it, and are exasperated trying to figure out what to do. So they do what they think is right and end up being sued.[4]

   The solution: Contract review and approval is just left to the lawyers, but is pushed to the relevant operating business unit to approve the commitment being made by that business unit, answering the question "Can you do what you are promising to do?" If there is a technical component to the promise to perform, a technical representative has to affirmatively answer the same question. Someone from Finance has to answer the question regarding the acceptability of price in light of expected margins. And, finally, the law department reviews to determine whether the risk ("Will we accept unlimited consequential damages?"), dispute resolution and other legal provisions are acceptable. This review process should, of course, then inform the contract drafting process. The review by the operating business unit is the most important because a contract that is properly performed hardly ever results in a dispute, which is the cornerstone of review by legal.

The largest example of line erasure is technology. Some talk about "legal technology", but technology has no unique link to law, and technology applied to problems that involve legal issues is no different than other technology. Take basic contract review technology that reviews documents to find out if the provisions of a contract conform to approved standards. There is nothing legal about this sophisticated word analytics.

The same features could be used to determine if a contract conforms to technical or operating standards. Artificial Intelligence may help companies evaluate data that could have implications for HR conduct that reduces the number of claims. While the tech may be legal in that it reduces claims, it is also HR tech that drives better conduct, helps improve hiring decisions and so on. The categorical adjective applied to tech puts guardrails around tech that it neither needs nor desires.

## What does all this mean for the legal vertical?

In short, the trends suggest an existential threat to the vertical aspect of legal. The lines that define the legal vertical are disappearing, right now, in real time, before our eyes. We have learned that despite the engineering precision with which the profession has created these lines, they are blurring and will eventually vanish. We know that in life, very little is black or white. Much of life is lived in shades of gray. And while the lines that define the legal vertical seem precise and straight, the edges of the lines are blurry and the path of the line is not straight. Shades of gray.

The lines were intended to serve a different purpose. People fear crossing lines, of invading another's territory or having someone else invade our space. These lines create comfort for us, providing an element of certainty we are each in our own space. We see this in the guild mentality of lawyers, especially with regard to non-lawyer ownership of law firms. It doesn't matter that expanding those who can be involved in the practice of law is good for clients. It is perceived as hurting lawyers and law firms, so the guild must resist.

Mark Cohen, an insightful commentator on the state of the profession, recently wrote:

> *Service providers tend to be more client-centric than law firms; they do not gauge success by profit-per-partner (PPP) because there are no partners. They have a corporate structure and, unlike law firms whose approach to legal delivery has remained largely static, service providers offer a seat at the management table for technologists and business experts as well as lawyers. This inter-disciplinary approach to legal delivery plus investment in technology and process has enabled them to steadily gain larger market share and to migrate up the complexity chain of outsourced tasks.*[5]

The first line is the key – law companies focus on their clients, law departments. Law firms actually focus on their clients too, but their real clients are the partners who conduct their own individual practices out of law firm space. Law firms are, in fact, akin to hotels for partners. You learn this as an associate when the way you do something for Partner A differs from the way you do the same thing for Partner B.

The other factor favoring law companies is their business model. The chosen business model for law firms creates disincentives for investment, including investment in technology for law departments and their own workflows. Law companies, on the other hand, use a standard business model, where the desire to grow enterprise value leads to significant investment in developing products in collaboration with their law department customers. The residents of the law firm hotels receive every comfort imaginable to justify the exorbitant rent, while law companies are focused relentlessly on reducing the cost of production and investing in tools that increase service velocity and quality.

But, as with many things today, the business world doesn't particularly care about lawyers' comfort. It does not care about the lines. When problems arise, there is no time to debate whether it is a legal problem or not. Nor is there value to doing so. The problem simply needs to be solved, effectively, swiftly and as cheaply as possible. This need does not mesh well with "the legal vertical". It meshes effectively with multi-disciplinary problem solvers, another factor favoring the rise of multi-disciplinary law companies.

## Conclusion

Lawyers are now challenged to move beyond just the law – because the problems have moved beyond just the lawyers. There is always, to be sure, an anecdote or two of a firm that "gets it", and many will take comfort in those anecdotes. The march toward the elimination of the lines on which the legal vertical has been built is inexorable. Too often, however, firms and their partners are focused on fighting today's fires rather than changing to meet looming demands. And that blind spot will be the undoing of many firms as the market shifts.

### *References*

1. Of the 30 companies on the Dow Jones Index, 22 were added after I began practicing law in 1982, 11 were added since 2000 and six were added this decade. www.fool.com/investing/2018/07/06/all-30-dow-stocks-ranked-by-tenure-in-the-index.aspx The turnover in the companies comprising the Fortune 500 is also an indicator of how much and how fast change is occurring.
2. www.altmanweil.com/dir_docs/resource/154F22DC-E519-4CE2-991D-492A0448C74F_document.pdf
3. www.bna.com/big-firms-plot-n73014477247/

4. In my 35 years litigating commercial disputes, I can no longer estimate the number of times this scenario has played out in one form or another.
5. http://legalmosaic.wpengine.com/wp-content/uploads/2016/02/LegalMosaic-final.pdf

# Chapter 3: The Big Four and the legal sector – what it means for law firms

*By Matthew Kellett, partner – UK law leader, Financial Services, EY*

The global legal market was valued at $600 billion in 2016.[1] Alongside the usual acquisitions and mergers, a new entrant has set its sights on the sector – the world's four largest consulting and audit firms, collectively known as the Big Four – looking to tap into this valuable market. According to a recent study, the Big Four – consisting of Deloitte, PwC, KPMG and EY – could draw an annual revenue of $30 billion from legal services, were they to fully expand into the market.

Presently averaging 2,200 lawyers in 72 countries, the Big Four are numerically on a par with large law firms such as Clifford Chance. It is therefore no surprise that 48 percent of law firm leaders believe that the Big Four are well positioned to make in-roads into the market, particularly with large financial services organisations and multi-national corporates.

The Big Four's legal divisions are already larger than most law firms and an enlarged workforce is one major route to winning over new clients. Deloitte has around 2,000 lawyers, while PwC over 3,500. If defined by headcount alone, hypothetically this would already make PwC a top 10 firm.

In recent years, all four of the accounting giants in the UK have begun to dip their toe back into the legal sector. Taking advantage of their scale and reach, and an increasing desire from clients for more streamlined and integrated services, the Big Four are ideally placed to enter the market.

EY is one of the largest multinational professional services firms in the world and has its own law division – EY Law.

In this chapter, Matthew Kellett, partner – head of law for financial services in the UK – shares personal reflections on how to build a Big Four legal practice, from scratch, and where this might lead in the future. This chapter represents the author's personal views, and do not constitute those of EY or any member firm.

## Overview

Having been a partner in both the Magic Circle and Silver Circle, as well as running a business in a bank, I knew the Big Four challenge would be different again. It was and, as ever, not always in the way I imagined.

This chapter discusses strategy, the first 90 days, culture and understanding, "Go-To-Market", the particular challenges of a Big Four platform, the huge advantages of the platform and whether, more broadly, lawyers in private practice should care.

## Strategy

Fundamentally, the overarching strategy of the Big Four is growth. When I joined EY in the UK Financial Services Organization in 2014 there was no specific business plan or strategy for the team. In fact, it was just me, a laptop and phone, and we were still waiting for the ABS license from the SRA – quite a change from approximately 40 partners in my department in my previous role.

Developing the strategy, I first set an objective that I thought we could achieve in a reasonable time frame – to be the leading Big Four legal team in the financial services sector in the UK.

I had five guiding principles:

1. Build a legal practice aligned closely to what the Financial Services business more broadly was known for – the risk and regulatory agenda;
2. Be relevant quickly – to clients and senior management;
3. Don't compete directly with the leading law firms – they are very good at what they do;
4. To harness the power of the EY sales machine: and
5. Big Four law should become its own sector in law.

Having set a goal and some guiding principles, I set about building the business.

It's a cliché, but differentiation really is the key. The practice had to provide something clients wanted and weren't getting from other suppliers. As a buyer of legal services myself, I'd seen too many lookalikes. It also needed to align closely to the wider business, both in terms of skills and client focus.

We built three offerings:

1. An agile Financial Service Regulatory team covering all FS sectors – to align precisely with the rest of EY FS's offering (and capture the "missing" 10 percent of engagements that go to outside counsel);
2. A market-leading legal risk consultancy – to straddle the law/consultancy divide (this morphed to include Legal Transformation, helping GCs make legal departments ready for the evolving challenge of managing legal risk and implications of technology on legal operating models); and
3. Legal managed services. This was focused on "routine and predictable" legal work, often using AI where large review exercises were required. This ultimately led indirectly to the acquisition of Riverview Law and our most significant growth opportunity.

They are diverse offerings on the face of it, but were targeted precisely at what FS clients weren't getting elsewhere and, given the wider brand strength, well received by the target market.

In contrast to traditional suppliers, we created a full end-to-end service (so we stayed involved where engagements ran for years). The other differentiator was that it was truly multi-disciplinary. Legal advice is integrated with non-legal advice. Less risk for clients (as suppliers hand work off to each other) and a more "holistic" product.

Big Four is very largely advisory, whilst law firms are transactional or event-driven. This strategy meant our practice was advisory and fitted more easily onto the EY platform. We then needed to harness the formidable sales or "go-to-market" infrastructure.

I consciously hired lawyers who could communicate well with non-lawyers (i.e. had the legal skills and quality but didn't wear their law on their sleeves). This was because it was important to dispel any negative stereotypes of lawyers and the wider legal profession, and to underscore the message that the team was an integrated part of a larger diverse team. One of my first hires was a business development director whose sole job was to connect us to the large account and business development teams as there weren't enough of us in the team to do this ourselves initially.

There seems to be a widely held belief (especially amongst lawyers) that every penny we make comes out of the pockets of private practice law, but I realized pretty quickly that our offering meant the opposite – it's not a zero sum game. Much of our growth came from work that would not have been "outsourced" and sometimes it was even work that wouldn't have been done at all, especially as the use of AI made work economic that hadn't been before. Our acquisition of Riverview Law, for example, supports the expansion of EY Law legal managed services globally and extends the existing EY Law offering, adding talent in legal innovation and operating model transformation, as well as further driving the current EY technology approach to legal managed services.

## Challenges

As with any job, you don't get a second chance to make a first impression. It's basic, but identifying key stakeholders, and getting buy-in on strategy as soon as possible was vital. Naturally, Big Four law has its own challenges. In particular, misunderstanding of lawyers' roles and skill sets and skepticism about the value they bring.

Misunderstanding was unexpected. Whilst the EY Leadership were in little doubt, at an operational level many colleagues wondered what we could add and skeptical as to whether clients would want to work with us. We "solutions" our offering, embedding our skills within wider EY client solutions – we literally becoming part of the solution.

Skepticism is often to be expected, especially given that lawyers and other Big Four professionals can, to the untrained eye, seem to be poles apart. The only way to grow is to win the hearts and minds of colleagues and develop trust and respect based on working together.

There was also a certain degree of suspicion initially, as it became apparent that there were lots of "near-law" businesses who saw us as competitors (and ones who could go further and deeper). This was more apparent than real, as most of their engagements included external lawyers, and with careful positioning and growing experience they realized we were additive. Also, looking at everything (e.g. a new regulation) through the lens of "contracts" meant we found some blue ocean in a very crowded organization as reviewing legal contracts is a bright line non-legal colleagues won't cross.

There are of course other challenges related to the size of the team and relevance to senior management in their day-to-day (rather than strategic) priorities, but since they are not unique to the Big Four I won't consider them further here.

## Advantages

Big Four is an unusual environment for lawyers, but there are advantages, not all of which are obvious until you're there.

Client relationships is probably the most striking. The sheer depth and breadth of client relationships is many times the size of even the deepest and most lucrative law firm relationships. This means there are a huge number of entry points into client organizations, which in turn means much greater opportunity – whilst most law firms are still anchored firmly to the general counsel's office in their sales efforts, the range of options for Big Four is much more extensive.

Once we had won the confidence of the dedicated client account teams to get them to sell our team to clients, it was more of a challenge to meet the demand from those teams for meetings with clients than having to push them for introductions. We were often meeting individuals who had very little or nothing to do with external legal suppliers, but saw the value of embedding legal advice alongside their other Big Four needs.

Given the importance of those relationships (given their size) the amount of daily contact with clients is enormous, as is the level of access to the client's senior people. For us, the art was to pick the meetings and introductions we wanted as carefully as possible (to avoid being stretched too thinly). Frankly it is quite something to behold when the sales force of the organization move into action. Of course, in a growing business they want to take every opportunity to increase their share of clients' spend and a new service like law is a great way to do it.

The depth of sector knowledge that the firm has should not be underestimated – there's an astonishing level of understanding of clients (as institutions) and their sectors. This comes out of the sheer level of interactions across a given sector, and a culture that "gets" that the best way to win work is to truly understand clients' issues at both the sector and organizational level. In the vast majority of cases there's a level of active listening and desire to understand clients' needs that is rarely seen in private practice, and from my own experience of some of the world's leading law firms pitching their wares to me when I was a buyer of legal services. It may be something to do with the way in which Big Four touch so many aspects of clients' businesses and then bring that together to get a holistic understanding.

Lawyers in law firms all too often see themselves as the center of the client's world, rather than just part of an overall goal or "a necessary evil". Being part of a truly multi-disciplinary team sets clients' legal issues in context and enables a better understanding of their relative importance. All too often, legal issues can be the tail wagging the dog, and clients do not in my experience take kindly to that. To be able to give a client a single document with legal and other advice embedded means law fits less obtrusively into the bigger picture. By the way, that document should always be PowerPoint or Excel, never Word!

For those seeking a career in a diverse environment, the Big Four are much more diverse than the vast private practice law firms, whichever criteria you use. I include that as a distinct advantage of the Big Four platform.

## The future

I'm often challenged as to whether lawyers should care about the rise of Big Four law? The simple answer to that is yes. The legal profession is changing fundamentally and the Big Four being back in law in the UK is one facet of that.

I won't rehearse the litany of well-known drivers of change, but in particular cost pressure, regulatory intervention, and technology all play into this. Buyers and sellers of legal services need to adapt, reluctantly or otherwise. However, I don't see leading law firms being cut out or gobbled up by the Big Four any time soon. Our business is not event-driven in the way most law firms are. We align with core business and solutions to offer a holistic solution. Our goal is client service, not "taking out" law firms. Too many just see competition rather than differentiation or opportunity. In time, I expect that will lead to Big Four law as a separate identifiable sector in law. This is fundamental if we are to succeed in the long term. Law firms will undoubtedly experience change in business and delivery models, but that isn't an impact per se of Big Four law. Big Four law may be a symptom but it is not the cause. Similarly, in-house counsel will experience change, but very little due to Big Four law. The main area of influence will be in the nascent legal managed services market.

Big Four law doesn't need to grow at the expense of private practice law. It is becoming a separate sector based on meeting clients' needs in new ways – truly multi-disciplinary. Technology is bringing new opportunities and at the same time increasing demand – which means there's still room for traditional players and new entrants.

If our only goal was to replicate existing private practice legal offerings we would fail – and that's not the plan. Ultimately this is not a zero sum game, and there will be plenty of room for all, but we will all have to adapt to the changing market.

### *Reference*

1. www.globallegalpost.com/big-stories/global-legal-services-market-valued-at-nearly-$600-billion-83628467/

# Chapter 4:
# Practical challenges for a multi-disciplinary practice

*By Rachel Khiara, Khiara Law*

This chapter's focus is on multidisciplinary practices in the UK, the practical challenges from a regulatory perspective, such as SRA jurisdiction, regulatory conflicts, and the complex position of lawyers and non-lawyers delivering client services jointly as part of a team, and the issue of legal professional privilege to the extent that it is available under the Legal Services Act 2007. The chapter provides some practical advice for the statutory compliance officers and their responsibilities, as well as lessons that can be learned for those in jurisdictions outside of the UK.

## Background

To give some context to the licensing and operational aspects of a multidisciplinary practice, it is necessary to consider the evolution of the licensing process in the UK.

In his report[1] on the regulation of legal services in the UK in 2014, Sir David Clementi recommended opening the legal services market to non-lawyer owners and managers, paving the way for new entrants into the market, offering a better choice for consumers and in so doing securing wider access to justice. One of the most beneficial structures recommended in the Clementi Report was the formation of multidisciplinary practices; "one-stop shops" where consumers could access their professional advisors in one place – for example, local law firms and local accountants servicing the needs of businesses through one company in an integrated and holistic offering.

Liberalization of the legal services market in the UK offered the Big Four access to a new market offering, allowing them to reposition themselves as broader advisors to their clients. Their audit work was becoming increasingly commoditized, and subject to considerable pricing pressure, and so it was necessary for them to broaden their horizons and look at multidisciplinary practice as solution.

KPMG became the first to gain authorization as an MDP regulated by the SRA in October 2014, swiftly followed by EY, and then PwC fully integrated its legal practice (previously housed in its subsidiary PwC Legal LLP) with the main firm, and earlier in 2018, Deloitte become the last of the Big Four to join. Their "non-practicing" solicitors were already in place, and now able to offer the full raft of legal services on authorization. Businesses worth millions of pounds were established overnight.

What is interesting is the approach of the firms and their ambitions. Despite the hype, all are insistent that they are not seeking to "compete" as a full service law firm, rather to offer integrated legal services and an holistic offering to meet their clients' needs and, where appropriate, work alongside a client's existing legal advisor. The legal services offered by the Big Four very much reflect the core practices of the firm.

And yet, despite this insistence, the Big Four are ranked alongside standalone firms in the Legal Directories. PwC, for example, has UK practices ranked tier one to three in *The Legal 500*, including commercial property, data protection, IT and telecoms, tax litigation and investigations, corporate crime, immigration, and M&A (smaller deals), with the latter two practices banded tier one. They also boast a raft of major clients to rival those of their City competitors. No law firm should be complacent.

The Big Four also illustrate a shift in the way in which legal services are delivered in the UK, which has generally seen the arrival of innovative and disruptive law firms. MDPs and AI are most likely to hit the mid-market hard, and this is where the Big Four will make their mark. The Big Four are not looking to compete with the Magic Circle, on whose referrals in the audit sector they frequently rely, but in the mid-market, the Big Four can deliver volume, automation, AI technology, and a global footprint that is far beyond that of most of those firms below the top 20.

## Licensing alternative business structures

Given the power of this offering, it is somewhat surprising that it wasn't until nearly three years after the Solicitors Regulation Authority had the power to license alternative business structures, that the first MDP (KPMG) was authorized. The truth of the matter was that to determine the SRA's regulatory jurisdiction in a multi-regulated vehicle, the complexities of teams of lawyers and non-lawyers working on the same matter, and dealing with regulatory conflicts, was simply filed on the "too difficult" pile, forcing PwC (which was looking to benefit early from the possibility of MDP) to settle initially for synthetic integration through a subsidiary vehicle.

At the outset, the primary concern in relation to the regulation of MDPs was the perceived scope of the SRA's jurisdiction, and critically the assumption that SRA regulation automatically extends, not just to the "reserved legal activities" set out in section 12(1), but to all "legal activities" as defined in section 12(3) of the Legal Services Act 2007. Those sections provide as follows:

*Section 12(1)*
*In this Act "reserved legal activity" means:*
*a) The exercise of a right of audience;*
*b) The conduct of litigation;*
*c) Reserved instrument activities;*
*d) Probate activities;*
*e) Notarial activities; and*
*f) The administration of oaths."*

*Section12(3)*
*In this Act "legal activity" means:*
*a) An activity which is a reserved legal activity within the meaning of this Act as originally enacted; and*
*b) Any other activity which consists of one or both of the following—*
*(i) the provision of legal advice or assistance in connection with the application of the law or with any form of resolution of legal disputes; and*
*(ii) the provision of representation in connection with any matter concerning the application of the law or any form of resolution of legal disputes."*

Given the breadth of the definition of the "legal activity", many activities undertaken by professional firms could be so classified, and in the particular instance of accounting MDPs, tax advice (which involves assistance in connection with the application of the law (i.e. the Taxes Acts)) would fall within that definition and should be SRA regulated, whether or not it is performed by lawyers. This gave rise to a host of problematic issues, such as dual regulation of individuals, insurance coverage, SRA fees on turnover, tighter rules on conflicts to name but a few, and would have had such adverse financial and regulatory consequences as would make regulation as an MDP an unfeasible proposition.

Even conceding that the work of non-lawyers would fall outside SRA regulation, this did not resolve the complex issue of mixed service lines – where the team comprises the non-lawyers and lawyers, but where the predominant service (as understood from a client perspective) may be *either* "tax and accounting services" *or* "legal services".

Turning therefore to the practicalities of operating an MDP, under the current SRA MDP Policy, within an MDP, the SRA regulates both personnel, and service lines. The regulated persons being all solicitors individually, the MDP itself (to the extent of the application of SRA professional principles and authorization requirements, such as the terms of the MDP's licence) and the statutory compliance officers who have responsibility for the legal services business only.

Of the services regulated by the SRA in an MDP, these include "reserved legal activity" and immigration work, and activities integral to those workstreams; non-reserved legal activity carried out by a non-lawyer unless such work is either subsidiary or necessary to the work of a non-lawyer or the matter is subject to suitable external regulation (such as the regulatory regimes of the ICAEW and FCA), or falls within an exemption for work supervised by a non-lawyer.

Looking at the MDP policy in more detail as a matter of practice, examples of those workstreams which are considered to be "integral" to reserved legal activity or immigration work (whether conducted by lawyers or non-lawyers) could include advice on liability or quantum where the MDP conducts litigation, or providing employment advice on a client's right to enter or remain in the UK when the MDP is acting for the client in relation to the visa application.

Under the MDP policy, the SRA's jurisdiction does extend to the work of non-lawyers, although in practice, the work is invariably covered by an exclusion from SRA regulation. Generally speaking, the work of non-lawyers in an MDP will be subsidiary but necessary to their role (this would cover, for instance, the work of tax advisors), or the work would be considered as regulated by suitable external regulation, whose regimes are deemed to be compliant with the SRA principles. The caveat is that in an MDP, where the work could be undertaken by a lawyer, regard should be had to client perception – is the client buying a legal service? this may well be the case where the legal work is extensive – and consideration given to whether the work been conducted by a non-lawyer in the past, in which case the client might expect the same regulatory treatment, or whether in fact the legal activity conducted by the non-lawyer is in fact integral to a reserved legal activity or immigration matter.

Turning to the difficult issue of the regulation of mixed teams of lawyers and non-lawyers advising on the same matter, the engagement will be SRA regulated unless the work is carried out under the direction and supervision of a non-lawyer, no reserved legal services are being conducted in the same matter (even if under a separate engagement), and no client monies are held on that matter. For this purpose, "supervision" means that the non-authorized individual is responsible for managing the risk on the engagement and is personally competent to oversee and supervise the services being delivered. This does not mean that the non-lawyer must have the expertise to provide the legal advice, provided that from a risk perspective, the non-lawyer is ultimately responsible for the advice given by the specialist to whom the legal activity has been delegated.

It is important to identify a client engagement as either an SRA or ICAEW regulated matter, to ensure that clients are afforded the correct regulatory protection. On an SRA regulated matter, there is a £3m minimum liability limit per single claim, which is generally much higher than that given in the ordinary course of an accounting firm's business. In addition, client records are retained for longer and there are specific client protections in place in relation to conflicts of interests, the termination of the retainer, complaints notifications, and disclosure of referral fees. The client will also benefit from SRA qualifying insurance policies.

The issue of conflicts of interests also raises interesting challenges in the context of an MDP. Under the SRA conflicts rules, lawyers cannot act where there is an "own interest" conflict, or where there is a client conflict, unless there is a common interest or the clients are competing for same objective and (i) they have given informed consent, (ii) there is a benefit to clients acting on both sides, and (iii) the SRA principles not breached. The conflicts rules in the ICAEW context differ as client protection is approached differently under the ICAEW regime. So, in the case of an own interest conflict or a client conflict, on an ICAEW matter, it is possible to act if (i) the client has given informed consent (ii) the risks of prejudice have been minimized, and (iii) safeguards are in place. In this regard, it is also important to note the regulators' views on "informed consent". The ICAEW is satisfied that it has given "informed consent" where permission to act in a conflict situation has been given in the engagement letter or as part of the MDP's terms of business, whereas for the SRA, the informed consent should be given at the time the conflict arises. This may not necessarily take the form of written consent, but any record of a conversation noting the consent should be retained.

In practice, the conflicts rules under the dual regime operate such that the SRA conflicts rules will only apply to a conflict with two SRA matters. In all other instances, even where one of the matters is SRA regulated, or there are lawyers on a mixed teams matter regulated by the ICAEW, the ICAEW conflicts rules will apply. In terms of lawyers involved in such matters, the ICAEW regime is assumed to provide sufficient protection, provided that solicitors will, in addition, be required to comply with the SRA principles, giving consideration as to where continuing to act would be in the best interests of the client, whether they could be said to be acting with independence. The solicitor on the mixed teams matter in an ICAEW conflicts situation will also need to be satisfied that the client has given informed consent and safeguards are in place. For this purpose, the informed consent should meet the SRA standard; a general term in an engagement letter may not suffice.

## Legal privilege

One particular area of interest in an MDP relates to the availability of legal professional privilege; originally the preserve of law firms and often used by law firm as a key benefit to a client. However, whilst the availability of legal advisory privilege is conferred by common law and the Solicitors Act 1974, in relation to alternative business structures in the legal services market (licensed bodied, for the purposes of the Legal Services Act 2007), such as MDPs, legal professional privilege is available pursuant to section 190 of the Legal Services Act 2007. The drafting of that section is not the clearest, so it is best set out in full:

> *Section 190(3) Subsection (4) applies where:*
> - *a) A licensed body provides services to a client; and*
> - *b) the individual ("E") through whom the body provides those services:*
>   - *(i) is a relevant lawyer, or*
>   - *(ii) acts at the direction and under the supervision of a relevant lawyer ("the supervisor").*
>
> *(4) Any communication, document, material or information relating to the provision of the services in question is privileged from disclosure only if, and to the extent that, it would have been privileged from disclosure if:*
> - *a) The services had been provided by E or, if E is not a relevant lawyer, by the supervisor; and*
> - *b) At all material times the client had been the client of E or, if E is not a relevant lawyer."*

Given the lack of clarity from the courts on the issues of legal privilege in licensed bodies, at this stage MDPs should proceed with caution in offering privilege to clients, particularly in teams of lawyers and non-lawyers. It is safest to assume, and to so provide in terms of business, that legal professional privilege will not automatically be available.

In practical terms, it is clear that privilege will only be available on SRA regulated matters, led by a lawyer (including a solicitor, barrister, equivalent in Scotland and NI, RFLs, RELs and certain legal professionals) who provides active supervision and direction. To demonstrate this, legal correspondence should be sent out in the name of the lawyer supervisor or another senior lawyer. Any advice given by non-lawyers, even where they are competent to do so, should be treated as provisional advice until subsequently confirmed in writing by the supervising lawyer. A lawyer working on the matter should ideally attend all meetings and calls, or be sent minutes of meetings and calls for their approval.

Circulation of information on a privileged client matter outside of the core advisory team is likely to cause privilege to be lost, and MDPs should be clear that privilege belongs to the client. This position should be explained to clients at the outset, to avoid the client itself inadvertently losing privilege by circulating privileged material to advisors elsewhere in the firm.

## Statutory compliance officer duties

Finally for consideration in this chapter are the obligations for the firm's statutory compliance officers – the compliance officer for legal practice (COLP) and the compliance officer for finance and administration (COFA). The roles of COLP and COFA are a fundamental part of a firm's compliance and governance arrangements. The COLP must be a lawyer, and is responsible for regulatory arrangements, and the COFA is responsible for compliance with the SRA Accounts Rules. In each case, the person designated as its COLP or COFA must be of sufficient seniority, in a position of sufficient power and responsibility, and have clear reporting lines to enable them to have access to all management systems and arrangements. In an MDP, the COLP's jurisdiction extends only to the MDP itself, in relation to the terms of its licence, SRA regulated matters, and lawyers within the MDP. Breaches of other regulators' regimes are not the responsibility of the COLP, save to the extent that it impacts on the legal business itself, for example, reputational issues.

Under rules 8.2 to 8.5 of the SRA Authorization Rules, COLPs' and COFAs' ability to take the steps they need to ensure compliance is dependent on the firm having suitable arrangements in place to ensure compliance with the terms and conditions of authorization, ensure compliance with statutory obligations, and record any failure so to comply and make such records available to the SRA on request. As the SRA regulatory regime is risk-based, or outcomes-focused, the extent of the systems necessary to demonstrate discharge of their personal responsibilities will depend on factors such as the size and nature of the firm, its work and its areas of risk. Compliance is also an ongoing responsibility and should be reviewed regularly. The SRA recommend, for example:

- Clearly defined governance arrangements providing a transparent framework for responsibilities within the firm;
- Appropriate accounting procedures;
- A system for ensuring that only the appropriate people authorize payments from client account;
- A system for ensuring that undertakings are given only when intended, and compliance with them is monitored and enforced;
- Appropriate checks on new staff or contractors;
- A system for ensuring that basic regulatory deadlines are not missed e.g. submission of the firm's accountant's report where the firm holds client monies, arranging indemnity cover, renewal of practising certificates and provision of regulatory information;
- A system for monitoring, reviewing, and managing risks;
- Ensuring that issues of conduct are given appropriate weight in decisions the firm takes, whether on client matters or firm-based issues such as funding;
- File reviews;
- Appropriate systems for supporting the development and training of staff; and
- Arrangements to ensure that any duties to clients and others are fully met even when staff are absent.

As soon as reasonably practicable, in the event of a compliance breach, the COLP or COFA is obliged to report to the SRA any material failure to comply, whether such failure is material either on its own or because it forms part of a pattern of non-compliance. The immediacy of the report will depend on the circumstances and seriousness of the breach. In considering whether a failure is "material", the COLP or COFA, as appropriate, will need to take account of various factors, such as:

- The detriment, or risk of detriment, to clients;
- The extent of any risk of loss of confidence in the firm or in the provision of legal services;

- The scale of the issue; and
- The overall impact on the firm, its clients and third parties.

Although it will commonly be appropriate for the firm to take steps to remedy breaches immediately, this does not obviate the need for compliance officers to record the breach and make a report to the SRA where appropriate.

Where, considering the factors above, the regulatory breach is "non-material", the COLP/COFA will need to keep appropriate records of failures. The SRA may ask for disclosure of these records, but in any event, they will be key to the work of the COLP and COFA in order to monitor regulatory compliance, and the efficacy of the firm's systems.

The practical aspects of operating as an MDP has significant benefits under the SRA regime, as it restricts the ambit of the SRA's regulatory jurisdiction. The so-called "Big Four" accountants have all entered the UK legal services market, evidencing consumer demand.

Law has traditionally been an insular profession in the UK. Success is measured by the development of expertise and accumulation of knowledge. However, there is a growing realization that there are systemic inefficiencies, and that law may be processed – broken down to component parts – whatever size or nature of matter. Law is, after all, a business. And this is where accountants have the head start. The strategic approach to delivery of services is completely different. Accountants are very good at project management, and have a much more widespread use of AI solutions and document automates.

Accounting firms have a proven track record of being able to capitalize on their brand and ability to deliver efficient services in order to establish new service lines; in the case of an MDP, legal services. Strategically, mid-sized firms may look to consider a merger with a similarly-placed accounting firm in the near future, in a market where differentiation in the middle market is key to success.

### *References*

1. www.avocatsparis.org/Presence_Internationale/Droit_homme/PDF/Rapport_Clementi.pdf

## Chapter 5:
# Strategic partnerships in law

*By Tony Young, partner, BDO*

The legal profession has always been slow to change – until now. Evolving client relationships, new technology, and an increased demand for connectivity are all having an impact on the profession, causing a faster pace of change than ever before.

Those working in the profession agree – the overwhelming majority (98 percent) of respondents to the 2017 BDO Law Firm Leadership Series study say that change in the legal industry is accelerating, with four out of five arguing the pace of change is significant.

The fast-moving nature of this change is leading to huge overhauls in the way law firms are structured. Even business models are changing as a result of disruption, with many considering a move to an IPO.

Put simply, this is a turning point for the profession. Law and professional service firms must learn to manage this change, or they will get left behind.

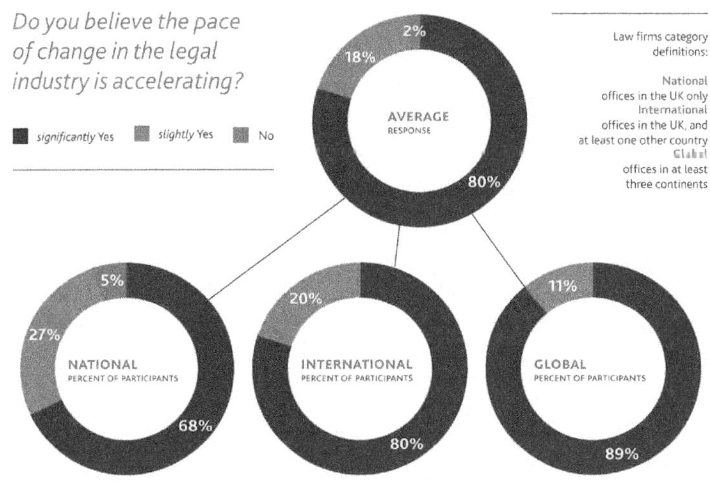


Source: Managing Rapid Change, BDO Law Firm Leadership Series 2017.

## Changing client relationships

Despite technological advances, what has fundamentally changed in the legal profession in the last 20 years is around the structure of the firm, compensation model, and billing structure. This all points to firms considering new client relationships where being an integral part of the team and not just a service provider will be key to future success and survival. Ultimately it is the responsibility of the law firm leaders to drive the internal changes needed to respond to these challenging external market forces.

Ten years on from the global financial crisis (GFC), the legal profession is still feeling the ramifications. The GFC signaled a profound change in client relationships – moving the power firmly into the clients' hands. Particularly over the past five years, we've seen clients' expectations around what law firms should be offering change significantly – and it's up to the firms themselves to keep up with this.

Legal professionals are no longer considered just a service provider – they are now expected to be an integral part of the team, finding ways to add value and support clients outside specific matters and even technical legal issues. Essentially, it's a matter of providing strategic partnerships instead of working on purely transactional engagements with clients.

But how can legal firms provide these functions? To be able to add value in the way clients have come to expect, it's essential law firms find a way to increase their connectivity and integration with the people they work with. In the BDO legal survey, we asked respondents to name what they expected to be the greatest change to how their firm works with clients in five years' time. The top responses were as follows:

- Greater connectivity and integration;
- New fees and fee arrangements;
- Greater collaboration between law firms, clients and third parties / more remote working and less face-to-face interaction (joint third);
- Closer relationships or partnerships;
- New ways of delivery service / greater transparency (joint sixth);
- More standardization / more international and global relationships (joint eighth); and
- New products and services.

The first – greater connectivity and integration – is not just limited to law, but has become an expectation for many clients across all industries.

To provide it, firms must offer clients more transparency and control, as well as providing for more collaborative ways of working. As with any current disruption, technology plays the starring role in enabling this.

The most successful firms will be those that position themselves to help their clients be successful in these increasingly challenging times. Greater collaboration between law firms, clients, and third parties is likely to be more complex than before, with clients driving this collaboration as they work with a greater range of providers. From a legal point of view, we are already seeing strategic moves with firms partnering with other disciplines (i.e. accounting firms) to go to market in a certain sector as a whole-service approach, or to address particular legislative or industry changes.

Still an under-used strategy, firms are introducing clients to other clients within the firm to create cross-fertilization. This approach has a low cost for acquisition and it is far easier to increase revenue from clients who already know and trust you. We are also seeing more firms forming alliances with industry bodies and participating in advisory boards for their clients.

## The impact of technology in law firms

Technological change is occurring across all industries – law is no different. The abundance of legal technology start-ups has made a huge range of different technologies available. What's different with this wave of technological change, however, is that it's no longer about increasing efficiency – it's about completely overhauling the way lawyers work. This is reflected in results from the BDO Law Firm Leadership Series – 94 percent of law firm leaders considered technology to be a strategic priority, whereas in the past many saw it merely as an operational matter.

Having said that, only six percent saw technological change as a top strategic priority, suggesting we are still some way away from fully utilizing the potential that technology can bring. This is despite the fact that technology plays a key role in supporting the new lawyer-client dynamic.

When it comes to providing greater connectivity and integration, technology can be used to:

- Provide new platforms for sharing files and data;
- Support greater use of law firms' client extranets and IT portals;
- Provide shared project management tools;

- Create collaborative online workspaces;
- Enable increased sharing of processes; and
- Increase efficiency across services.

Technology gives both clients and law firms direct access to the files they need. Increased visibility of a client's operations allows law firms to find those essential value adding elements that go beyond simply carrying out a set legal task for them. It also increases efficiency and transparency – no more long email chains or delays in providing essential documents. Instead, the information is all there in one place.

The converse of this is that, although there will be an increase in collaboration with clients, there will also be a decrease in the amount of face-to-face interaction involved. Some traditionalists may rue this, but it does present opportunities for law firms. Less time spent with clients and quicker completion of work due to file sharing arrangements means lawyers can now serve far more clients than they were previously able to. They can also potentially serve overseas clients (although this also means overseas firms can now serve them). The law firms that truly succeed will be the ones that find a way of adding a personal touch while also making use of the increased efficiency technology has enabled.

Of course, as with all technological change, there is also controversy. Will every new piece of technology provide improvements, or will some merely disrupt? Some are more inclined to believe the latter. One in five respondents to the BDO survey said Artificial Intelligence (AI) is likely to replace lawyers and revenue streams. In addition, they believed commoditization will create greater competition for specialist advice and consulting services.

While there is certainly some negativity, there is also a lot of optimism around what technology can bring to the legal profession. Yes, AI will replace many tasks that lawyers carry out, but this means they have more time to take on those complex, value-adding tasks that clients are demanding. Greater productivity and efficiency is also expected to refine processes and reduce production costs, while the new services and delivery models that technology enables give lawyers the ability to deliver much more in-depth analysis and new ways of charging for certain legal services. For example, there is a growing trend for in-house legal departments to turn to law firms for advice on management and operational issues, including new technology investments.

No discussion of technological change would be complete without the mention of data. Over the past ten to 15 years, digital data has exploded.

The use of email and an exponential increase in digital processes and documentation has transformed transactional due diligence and litigation discovery processes – and "data-driven law" is being talked about more and more. As with any data strategy, the aim is to provide far more insight than was ever previously available. Already, many law firms have hired data analysts and consultants to deal with this vast amount of information. They can analyze huge amounts of case law and legislation to quickly find relevant content for their own engagements.

### How can people and technology work together?

One of the greatest discussion points surrounding technology centers on what its impact will be on the professional workforce. Indeed, cultural change was named in the BDO survey as the greatest challenge law firms face in keeping up with technology. It's paramount that professional service firms are able to get their people on board with new technology. To do this, they must build a culture that supports experimentation and harnesses the different skill sets available across the workforce.

This is helped by the fact that there are currently five different generations in the workforce, all of which have vastly different attitudes towards technology. The youngest have grown up with technology as part of their daily lives. The oldest have seen it evolve, moving from the early fax machine to an age where AI has become common parlance.

If we are to truly embrace technology as a workforce, continuous learning will be essential. This must involve a recognition of people's own imperfections. Thomas DeLong, in a session given at the Harvard Business School in 2016, said he wants to see new graduates in professional service and law firms realize "they don't have to be their CV every day". They can be authentic, admit they are fallible and that there are things they need to learn. This is an excellent point, but it shouldn't just apply to younger graduates. In an age where technology is constantly changing and disruption is the rule, not the exception, we must all admit our knowledge gaps and be open to learning new things.

That said, for graduates, the ability to upskill and continuously learn may be more critical than for other generations. Most professional services firms have never really viewed IT as a core competency. However, now they are looking to simplify their IT capabilities through moving some processes to the cloud and streamlining their infrastructure – in many cases by outsourcing and offshoring. If AI or offshoring is going to take over some of the skills graduates are learning in tertiary studies, their ability to find new areas for study and upskilling will determine their survival in the profession.

Collaboration will be fundamental to enabling the type of continuous learning required in this age of technological disruption. Recent graduates have a lot to teach those in older age groups, indicating that reverse mentoring may be a positive route to take with regards to understanding how technology can shape and enhance their roles. Businesses across all industries need to ensure there is open communication between these generations. Again, technology (in the form of idea sharing platforms) will play an important role.

In addition, many professional services firms are using technology to ensure employees have access to the information and systems they need wherever they are and whenever they need it. This means they can perform their jobs to their full potential while still being flexible.

## In summary

To summarize, the legal profession is changing faster than ever. Client demands are growing – they now expect lawyers to find ways to add value outside of purely transactional engagements.

Technology will be the main way lawyers can provide this added value, creating opportunities for quicker and smoother collaboration and transparency. But this also means more competition among law firms – those that survive will be the ones that are able to keep the personal touch while still utilizing technology to the best of its ability.

To do this, professional service firms must find ways to enable people and technology to work together. Continuous learning will be essential to embracing the fast pace of change moving forward, as will taking advantage of the many different generations in the workplace to provide reverse mentoring. Again, technology provides a platform to assist with continuous learning, creating a collaborative space for the sharing of ideas.

Too many law firms have ignored change for too long. But in the modern business age, no industry exists in a bubble. Change is happening – you can either embrace it and turn it into an opportunity, or you can ignore it and let it become a disruption. The ball's in your court.

Chapter 6:

# How the pressures for new business models mean AFAs are finally coming of age

*By Chris Howe, Raedbora Consulting Ltd*

## Introduction

There have been many articles, books, and commentaries predicting the end of the hourly rate for legal work stretching back over some decades. I have been engaged with the legal sector for some 20 years now, following a successful career in consulting and the financial industry, and this has been a topic of debate for all of those years.

Some strides have been made, with fixed fees now commonplace in certain markets and sectors. However, truly innovative pricing has been largely absent and for good reason, despite the pundits' predictions.

This time, however, I think it will be different. The forces driving this change are largely external and diverse. Readers should note that when change comes it is likely to be rapid and many will be left stranded by the pace, like so many pebbles on the beach after the tide has gone out.

## The case for AFAs

A long-standing complaint from legal buyers has been around the extensive use of hourly rates for pricing legal work. Buyers argue that there is no clarity in advance of the cost of the job so no true ability to compare one supplier with another or the ability to assess whether to proceed or not based on cost. Additionally, the buyer has no effective insurance against a law firm who completes the job inefficiently either by taking too long, or using over-qualified resource. There is also no incentive to find new innovative ways of delivering the work as these tend to substitute hours booked by people with machines or computers, for which there is no charging mechanism.

For the lawyer, whose business depends heavily on skilled people, the hourly rate gave a simple means of pricing and billing work as well as some insurance against the frequent position whereby the client or a third party changed their requirements, thus extending the scope of work done. This is especially prevalent in legal and probably explains why the hourly rate has been so persistent. Clients would of course argue that this is simply the lawyer taking on no commercial risk whatsoever in the matter and expecting the client to pay, whatever the lawyer's performance or efficiency.

Accountants have been culpable in the widespread adoption of hourly rates. Cost rates for hours worked are a standard technique across industry, but in legal an additional slice is added for overheads, and further for profit to produce the hourly rate. In the process this gives the impression that profit and overhead increase linearly with hours worked. This makes life easy for the accountant as the true cost drivers for overhead and profit therefore no longer need close scrutiny, provided a certain number of hours and rate are achieved. However, it misleads the fee-earner tasked with winning work.

## Change to date

Buyers have been pressing for change for some time, with mixed results. It was thought that the recession of ten years ago and the consequent increase in buyer power would force change – and to a degree it has. The extent to which buyers still have the whip-hand varies by sector depending on supply of qualified lawyers, the volume of work the buyer has to award, and whether alternatives are available. It is certainly the case that buyers will no longer tolerate hourly rates for repeatable volume-based work.

Over the last ten years we have seen widespread adoption of fixed fees for certain forms of work. The typical criteria for the use of fixed fees are:

- Large number of small matters that are very similar. This allows the lawyer to be confident in their calculation of cost and so profit;
- Matters where technology/process approaches can be used. In these cases hourly rates were never a great guide as a significant proportion of the cost was not people related; and
- Competitive work. Where buyers have a clear choice of providers and the work is price-sensitive then those offering fixed fees have been preferred.

However, the change that has taken place is limited as follows:

- Any fixed fees quoted are usually based on and derived from an estimated figure itself derived from hourly rates; and

- More innovative arrangements are rare – perhaps only extending to cap and collar or variations of CFAs, themselves based on hourly rates.

The old business models for law firms are now under threat, however, and this may finally deliver the change we have been waiting for.

## What is different this time?

Ten years ago the argument was that buyers had control and so, in a market where supply exceeded demand, change would be forced through. It is certainly the case that prices came under pressure and in so-called commodity areas fixed fees have come to the fore. The more radical change expected has not transpired, however, with a few notable exceptions.

This time, there are multiple changes providing opportunities for the industry for those prepared to take them. These changes are:

- Price pressure continues in some areas;
- Technology plays an increasing part of delivery;
- AI promises radical changes to service delivery;
- Deregulation gathers pace; and
- Buyers look for deep integration into their own business models.

Let's take each briefly in turn.

### Price pressure

While it is true that supply and demand are more matched than in recent years, and some legal services have made progress on raising prices, many areas still experience a competitive environment. The legal industry has been slow to consolidate in comparison with, for example, accountancy; as a result there are many competing firms for big buyers to choose from. Buyers are consolidating their purchasing power both through their sheer scale and by restricting the size of their panels. The prize for successful firms is therefore ever larger, and the number of opportunities more restricted. Competition therefore remains fierce.

### Technology

Technology (i.e. computers) is replacing a greater proportion of legal hours over time. Starting at the low-value volume end of the market, this trend will stretch into higher value, more complex work over time.

Lawyers initially see this as a "value" opportunity to pitch to their clients, but tech is not free and in particular its costs do not vary well with volume, or hours worked by a human. Law firms will therefore quickly need to work out a business model that allows them to charge for the value created by their tech before they find they have given that value away. Firms should look to software vendors and content generators (such as film and TV) for suitable business models, and in this context it is worth reflecting how rapidly the model for firms delivering video content via cable or satellite is being eroded by new entrants using the internet to get their content to users directly.

## AI

There has been much discussion (perhaps hype) about the impact of AI on legal. AI formed part of my engineering degree 30 years ago and we should start by clarifying that none of what is currently being discussed is really AI as it would not pass the Turing test, which defines AI.[1]

The solutions we are seeing now might be better described as "learning programs", which develop their algorithms based on experience rather than direct programming. I have one that decides when to turn on my heating – an example that serves to illustrate the simple concept underlying these tools, and that that concept is a necessary but not a sufficient condition for AI.

However, the changes that are afoot are still very relevant. The new tech being labelled as AI is essentially delivering two key results:

- The ability to sift and review information and deliver conclusions that are as reliable or better than a qualified human can; and
- The ability to interact with a client (for example via an online questionnaire) to identify their requirements and issues.

The latter feature has been around for some time, but the sophistication of each of these aspects is increasing at a rapid pace and already these programs are beginning to replace humans from what would have previously been considered high-value roles not susceptible to replacement by machines. The risk here is simple – that rapidly swathes of what we currently consider high-value chargeable hours will be lost.

Taking technology and AI together, one can see that the hourly rate will quickly become unsustainable as the value delivered to clients will largely be a result of technology, not human hours. New business models are required.

### Deregulation

The traditional law firm is also under attack from alternative business structures (ABS), which allow others to enter the legal market via routes different to the traditional partner-based model.

Aside from increasing the pool of supply, some of these ABSs have business models much better suited to the new world where technology will be a large component of service delivery. Traditional law firms should aware that as new technology becomes established, these new firms may establish themselves and come to dominate.

### Deeper integration

Some of the more innovative legal deals of recent years (such as the Eversheds–Tyco arrangement and similar) point not just to a trend for reduction in the size of panels, and innovative pricing arrangements, but to a deeper change. These innovative deals rely on a very close integration between the client and the law firm, which can often only be achieved with one key provider, locking out the competition. This deeper integration can have the following features:

- Transfer of some functions to the law firm as an outsourced provider (e.g. the transfer of an entire legal function to be managed by the law firm on behalf of the client);
- Transfer of some functions to the client which may include scheduling, allocation of resources, a dedicated client team jointly managed; and
- Streamlined instructing and billing processes speeding up and simplifying start up, delivery and billing.

The benefits to clients and successful law firms are clear, but these models do require firms to be capable of operating different business models to suit their clients, not necessarily to suit the partners. All ideas of hourly rate are of course totally inappropriate for pricing such arrangements.

### How fast could change come?

Having talked about change for many years in the sector, readers could be forgiven for thinking "it will never happen". Certainly, the oft predicted consolidation of law firms has been very slow and continues at a sluggish pace when compared to other industries.

There are reasons, however, to think that the factors above will come together to drive much more rapid change this time around. Reference to other industries shows that once a key tipping point is reached, change can become rapid. A couple of examples may serve to illustrate.

### Retail – a case study

Retail has undergone significant change over the last five years, with more to come; this sector may be a harbinger of the changes we may see in legal.

Online sales as a proportion of total sales in the UK have shown an increase from around three percent in 2006 to around 18 percent in 2018.[2] That change has been steady without any sudden exponential growth. However, the impact has not been nearly as smooth and the change in shape of the market contains some useful pointers:

- Online retail started out with a wide range of online sellers, of which only a few have come to be prominent – such as Amazon;
- Traditional retailers opening online operations have also been successful, often keeping out new entrants by virtue of their trusted brand – all the key retailers now have online presence through the "bricks and clicks" model; and
- There is now too much physical retail space and a large number of stores and chains are now either closing or rapidly shrinking their high street presence.[3]

What we can learn from this:

- There will be some new entrants to legal; but
- Traditional firms that adapt can have a successful future if they adopt the new ways of working; and
- A point will be reached where rapid and significant shrinkage of the traditional models will be required. This will lead to some firms going out of business and others rapidly shrinking their traditional models.

### The rise of streaming services

No one can have missed the rise of players such as Amazon Prime, Spotify, Deezer and so on. These streaming services are growing rapidly, and it is worth reflecting on what distinguishes them from their competition (cable, satellite TV providers, radio, DVD, CD):

- Streaming services live or die by content. They are not distinguished by or as a means of distribution or channel, but the content they provide;
- Their business models are often simpler and more accessible for the user with no lock-in annual contracts; and
- The service can be received in a variety of ways but all utilising new communications technology – being internet via broadband or mobile.

As with the changes in retail, their growth has steadily developed over the last few years, but as with retail, a tipping point appears to have been reached with a rapidly increasing number of US consumers "cutting the cord" on their cable TV service.[4]

Both these examples illustrate that gradual change to a new business model can catch traditional players unawares. A point is reached where the traditional model is no longer sustainable, and businesses have to rapidly withdraw from their previously long-maintained business models. It is not yet clear just when this will happen in legal. What is clear, however, is that all the ingredients are present for change to come rapidly.

### How might the future look for legal?

This remains unclear, but I think we can suggest the following ingredients:

- There will always remain a small premium market for traditional-style legal advice. This will be for particularly tricky advice in specialist areas. Clients will be willing to pay premium prices for this work as the advice usually carries very high value. It is equally clear, however, that this market will be very small relative to what might currently be called "premium";
- Technology and AI will replace a large proportion of the work performed by most mainstream firms. As the technology improves, so does their ability to cope with a wider range of circumstances with reliability. Soon users will prefer to trust the computer's answer, at which point the switch over will become rapid;
- Alternative business models and therefore AFAs will become the norm because the traditional model will no longer reflect the law firm's mode of operation;

- Legal operations will become integrated between client and supplier in the way that many office services are. For example, front office, building support, security, and IT are often outsourced via a service agreement; and
- Payment by the hour will become largely irrelevant – not because clients demand the change but because neither party has any further use for it.

## Conclusion

After years of prevarication it now seems that the range of client and environmental pressures now building will finally force law firms to adopt AFAs as standard for most work. Ironically, the deciding factor is likely to be the impact of technology on business models, which will render the traditional *modus operandi* as obsolete as the typewriter. When the change comes it will be rapid and many will not have time to adapt.

Transformative change is now on the immediate horizon and, as ever, those who embrace it are likely to thrive.

### *References*

1. The Turing test, developed by Alan Turing in 1950, is a test of a machine's ability to exhibit intelligent behavior equivalent to, or indistinguishable from, that of a human - https://en.wikipedia.org/wiki/Turing_test. For an interesting illustration see the film "Ex Machina" – www.imdb.com/title/tt0470752/
2. ONS – www.ons.gov.uk/businessindustryandtrade/retailindustry/timeseries/j4mc/drsi
3. www.bbc.co.uk/news/business-45601853
4. www.zdnet.com/article/cord-cutting-picks-up-speed/

# Chapter 7:
# Business model transformation in an age of digital leverage

*By Robert Millard, partner, Cambridge Strategy Group*

A firm's *strategy* defines its future direction, essentially setting out the markets, the clients, and the services on which it intends to focus investment and effort. A firm's *business model* defines the combination of structures, systems, and processes by which it will achieve its strategic objectives, drive performance and otherwise meet the requirements of its owners. It describes the means by which the firm creates and delivers value to clients and captures value for itself. Finally, a firm's *business planning* involves the specific actions that the firm will take in order to achieve its strategic objectives and operate its business generally. This chapter focuses specifically on how law firm business models might evolve as the practice and the business of law becomes increasingly digitally-enabled and client legal needs also evolve as a result of similar pressures.

## Digital transformation

The strategy, business model, and business planning dimensions are frequently conflated, which causes confusion at a time when that is ill-affordable. In addition, straddling all three dimensions today is the process of *digital transformation* that is unfolding across many businesses, including the more progressive law firms. It makes little sense today to speak of any of these dimensions without including the opportunities and challenges presented by digital trends such as AI, distributed ledger technologies / blockchain, big data and the Internet of Things (IoT) that are emerging in what the World Economic Forum (WEF) calls the "Fourth Industrial Revolution". Law firms are certainly not immune to these trends, although the regulatory protection that they enjoy in some jurisdictions has been a useful buffer against them – at least in those jurisdictions. In some high-growth emerging markets, the effects are diluted also by supply and demand pressures being against the client and in favor of the law firms – not unlike the balance that existed in Europe and North America in the decade leading up to the global financial crisis in 2009. One has only to compare the day-to-day practice and business realities in most law firms today to what they were just a decade ago, to realize how much has changed. The sense that much more has yet to change is unavoidable, though. The drivers for change have manifested themselves in a number of ways, for instance:

- Unrelenting pressure on in-house departments to deliver "more for less" being passed on to external legal advisors;
- Hypercompetitive market for legal services in a relatively flat economy with high risk of recession;
- Legal work being taken in-house; the emerging threat of the "Big Four" global advisory firms and other alternative legal service providers;
- Increasing gap between what general counsels (GCs) want from their external legal advisors and what relationship partners think they want;
- Client conversations frequently get stuck at "more for less" and other tactical factors;
- Larger clients are reducing the number of law firms on their panels; and
- Obstacles to translating good ideas that emerge during client listening into viable projects at scale.

## The expectation gap between GCs and law firms

Many GCs complain today that what they are communicating during "client listening" exercises is not being translated into action by their law firms. A serious expectation gap has arisen. We believe that this gap points not to a breakdown in strategy, nor to a disregard on the part of law firms or their lawyers to their clients' needs/desires. Most lawyers, we believe, are genuinely anxious to serve their clients well. Instead, it points to corporate inertia in organizations that for many years have operated within a single, monolithic, highly successful business model, and the need now to transform that model to align with modern requirements. Clients are challenging law firms to reassess their value propositions (which are a key element of any business model) and to:

- Transition from technical legal expert to strategic legal advisor;
- Deliver more value and reduce costs through innovation and use of technology;
- Increase transparency and certainty of pricing and support GCs in meeting their budgets;
- Collaborate more closely with in-house legal teams;
- Unbundle work and source matters more intelligently, adopting tiered resourcing models;
- Invest in continuous relationships; and
- Understand emerging legal needs and help client legal teams understand their own strategic horizons.

The law firms that have failed utterly to meet these challenges probably no longer exist, but of those that remain in the market, many are hamstrung by trying to force-fit these new approaches into a business model that is effectively no longer fit for purpose.

### The "Tournament of Lawyers" business model and its origins

This monolithic law firm business model that thrived through most of the 20th century has a name. In 1992, it was dubbed the "Tournament of Lawyers" (ToL) in a book of that title by Galanter and Palay.[1] To discover the reasons why the ToL model is under pressure, one has to examine its own roots in another of the WEF's industrial revolutions, namely the second. This revolution occurred in the early 20th century, in response to fundamentally disruptive innovations that were invented in the late 19th century. The most transformational of these were the internal combustion engine, distributed electricity, and the telephone. Collectively, these technologies transformed modern society, business, and industry. This led to an exponential increase in the volume and complexity of law. Law firms had to bulk up and specialize more deeply, as a result. The demand for legal services and the need for a more sophisticated way of pricing as the business of law became more complex led to the leveraged "up or out" model of talent management, and the billable hour. Until the emergence of digital tools spawned by the invention of the personal computer and the world wide web (the WEF's third Industrial Revolution), the model was wildly successful.

Much ink has been spilt on the topic of the "law firm of the future" and how the fourth Industrial Revolution might impact legal services, generally. Scenarios have been sketched out of worlds where lawyers are replaced by robots or rendered otherwise redundant, or where the practice of law becomes so unprofitable that it becomes attractive to the caliber of intellects that make good lawyers, or where law firms become extinct and legal services are provided by what we now call "alternative legal service providers". These scenarios make for interesting speculative debate and media headlines, but they are of little value to firms trying to make sense of what they need to do, right now, to better align their business models with client needs – without going out of business by simply reducing price to levels that are unprofitable in their quest to deliver "more for less".

## Using business model transformation to bridge the GC expectation gap

This draws one back to the expectation gap that so many GCs have complained has arisen between them and their law firms, and that they say is growing wider. One is drawn inevitably to the conclusions that:

- Law firms need to better understand their clients' current and future needs and adapt accordingly if they are to maintain existing relationships, acquire new mandates, and differentiate themselves in an increasingly diverse and competitive legal services market;
- The embarkation point for any change program with a goal of improving client service has to start with deep consultation and collaboration between clients and key internal stakeholders to validate needs and proposed solutions. To do so otherwise is to set out on a high risk, high cost expedition without a map;
- Traditional client relationship management approaches are not delivering what clients need. Part of the problem has been the tendency to view client engagement on a transactional level, at the expense of the longer-term relationship view and a deeper understanding of the internal business drivers shaping GCs' needs. On the other hand, corporate legal departments have not necessarily been sufficiently proactive and coordinated in providing their law firms with the feedback and insights that will help them adapt effectively;
- Correcting this requires that deep insights be built through open dialogue and intense collaboration, combining features of Agile experimentation and Legal Design Thinking to develop highly informed, validated service innovations that will secure and

expand client relationships for the long-term. Solutions need to focus on four facets:

- Modify current services to better service existing client needs;
- Understand emergent client legal needs that create opportunities for new services;
- Modify service delivery channels to enhance efficiency and client experience; and
- Operational and organizational impacts for the law firm of adopting any solutions.

- Law firms need a far better understanding of their most important clients' perspectives on these issues. In-house teams need to better understand the practicalities from the law firm's perspective. Solutions that are developed collaboratively between law firms and their clients tend to be better focused, and both sides are invested in their success. This also has the added benefit of creating jointly-developed IP, entrenching collaborative approaches, and cementing relationships between law firms and in-house teams.

Once law firms and their clients have begun to understand the above and develop solutions, the law firms will have the information that they require to retool their business models, to align better with client needs, and at the same time optimize the economic performance of the business. Without that, the solutions agreed will frequently not be able to be optimized, or will fail completely, because the firms will be attempting to implement them within a business model that does not encourage that or, at worst, makes them impossible.

Approaching business model transformation from this perspective means that the challenges in focus move from being longer-term and debatable, to being immediate, definite, and of existential importance. And of existential importance they certainly are, over the strategic horizon of three to five years, for all but a handful of the most premium or specialized firms. As the ToL business model has come under pressure, so conventional law firms have lost market share to other kinds of legal service providers. Chief amongst these are clients themselves. In a world where businesses are outsourcing as many functions as possible, they have discovered that legal services are the one area where they can provide those services considerably cheaper internally, than by procuring them from external law firms.

Again, this points to failures far more in business model transformation than in strategy or business planning. On the fringes now are the "Big Four" global advisory firms and others, pitching value propositions to clients that they can take that work on at a price that is competitive, yet yields adequate profit for them. Digitally-enabled legal practice is key to these propositions.

## Will law firms be replaced by other legal service provider types?

Is it true that law firms as a business construct are unable to evolve, and are doomed? Will legal services in the future be dominated by entirely different kinds of legal service provider? Some point to Clayton Christensen's theory[2] of "disruptive innovation", first introduced in 1995, as evidence that the ToL model, and hence law firms as a construct, are largely doomed. It is dangerous to accept this premise at face value. "Disruption" is a term that is widely misused, frequently by people who have not applied more than the most superficial of critical thought to Christensen's theory and its applicability to the ToL model.

The essential flaw in their logic is that the theory is designed to describe the process whereby a new, better innovation that emerges entirely disrupts an industry because the incumbent leaders cannot evolve fast enough to compete with new entrants. It works very well in the technology industry, where a new technology frequently completely displaces an older technology and renders it obsolete. Vinyl records, for instance, were displaced by compact discs, then by mobile devices like MP3 players, then by streaming media. No such new innovation or business model has emerged in the legal industry, to fundamentally displace the ToL business model. Instead, what we are seeing is a steady evolution of that model, as technology proves capable of doing more and more work previously done by lawyers, more accurately and efficiently.

There is no doubt that new business models are emerging, but to supplement the ToL model rather than entirely replace it, at least at first. Within a few years the performance drivers in law firms will be very different to those that have been familiar in the past, and probably far more complex. The evolutional process is incremental rather than disruptive, though. It is unfolding in steps, rather than one big transformation. The appropriate strategy for addressing business model transformation is radically different, between disruptive and incremental change.

The real danger with incremental change is that it is less obvious, and the effects of avoiding it can be diluted until they manifest in a crisis. It may be argued that the reason why many law firms are under pressure today is because of simple resistance to change, failing to use strategies and technologies that are already available, in plain sight. Part of this may be a fear that what is required is a radical retooling of the entire firm, as would be necessary if the competing innovations were transformationally disruptive (as described by Christensen.) At the risk of repetition: while one should not discount the possibility that truly disruptive innovations will emerge at some point, at present they are incremental. This requires a different, more gradual and thoughtful approach to business model transformation.

It is highly likely that the leading law firms of the future will not have a single, monolithic model like ToL. Instead, in our view they will have more sophisticated, multi-faceted business models that align how different parts of the business are managed with the drivers of performance for each, in a far more granular fashion. It is easy to see this work well elsewhere in the market. Many large business enterprises in a wide range of industry sectors consist of many different kinds of business, each with their own performance drivers and customer segments, and their own business models that are each designed to extract the maximum value from each.

## Changing mindsets, behaviors, and cultures

The most fundamental changes that are required involve mindset, behavior and culture. Once progress is made with that, changes to structure, systems, and processes are far easier. Foremost amongst these is the need to move the firm-wide emphasis for how performance and success are measured from production- to value-based metrics. As a first step, firms need to move from emphasized revenues (especially those derived through hourly billing) to profit and client-focused metrics such as net promoter score (NPS). Without this, it will be extremely difficult for firms to diversify their models away from their relentless focus on hours worked and revenues billed and collected. Conversely, there seems no reason why law firms that can move beyond this should not be able to similarly diversify their portfolio of business models, delivering greater value to clients and capturing greater value themselves.

Yet another challenge exists, though. It is very difficult to transform a business model in any enterprise that is actively trading, given that one needs to balance the drivers of current performance with what needs to be done to effect change. The latter inevitably disrupts the former. It is therefore unsurprising that many of the legal service providers who are currently thriving are indeed new entrants to the market, or at least businesses that are radically scaling up their legal businesses.

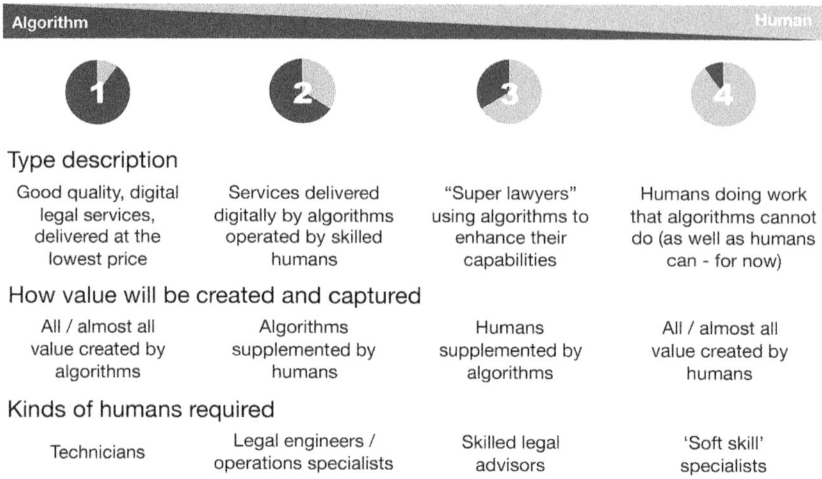


*Figure 1: The characteristics of different business models across a continuum ranging from where work is delivered entirely by human effort, to where it is delivered entirely by a technological platform. (Adapted from Agrawal, Gans and Goldfarb, 2018).*[3]

Firms pay a great deal of attention to ensuring that their partners and other senior leaders have a common understanding of the firm's strategy. Successfully transforming business models requires that as much attention be paid to a common understanding of the firm's performance drivers, too.

## Digitally-enabled law firms – a continuum of digital vs human value

In the first instance, let us focus on how value-creation and profit performance drivers vary across a continuum from where the work is delivered entirely by human effort, to where it is delivered entirely by a technological platform. This continuum is illustrated in Figure 1.

Type 4 is the model that prevails in the ToL model and that characterized law firms through much of the 20th century, and the first two decades of the 21st. Legal work product is generated almost exclusively by human effort, either by lawyers working alone or in leveraged teams consisting of partners, associates, and others. This model will likely continue to exist but, as technology becomes increasingly competent and commonplace, it will become limited to those areas of practice where the level of ambiguity and complexity makes humans better suited to the problem-solving required, than technology. For an indication of what legal work likely falls into this category, one should examine the work of Carl Frey and Michael

Osborne at the University of Oxford,[4] on which jobs that exist today could be at risk of being taken over by robotics or AI in the next 20 years. Their research concludes that the jobs least likely to be automated are those that require skills of creative intelligence, social intelligence, or physical dexterity. That certainly includes a great deal of high-end legal advisory work, so it is unsurprising that Frey and Osborne regard lawyers as one of the professions *least* likely to be displaced by technology.

What is clear though is that lawyers doing work that requires skills of creative intelligence and social intelligence (perhaps more than physical dexterity) will be required to deal with far more data in their work than before. The amount and the complexity of data involved in modern legal work involving the more difficult, important client challenges is increasing exponentially, with no indication that this trend will slow. At the same time, machine-learning technology (popularly termed artificial intelligence or AI) is becoming rapidly more adept at analyzing vast quantities of data, accurately and efficiently, and delivering a summary of salient issues to their users. Much has been written about these technologies and their ability to enable lawyers who use them to deliver a far more valuable service to clients. In Figure 1, this falls into Type 2. It is reasonable to expect that more and more work will move to this modality, especially high-end work. Leverage would be achieved through a combination of people and technology. A lawyer's skills would rely as much on her ability to use the digital tools effectively, as to apply her mind to the insights delivered by those tools. Firms would develop competitive advantage through the unique know-how developed through and within these tools, as well as the expertise of the people using them.

A point will come where it becomes difficult to distinguish between the value that is created by the lawyer, versus the digital tools that the lawyer delivers. For a parallel, consider the role of computer aided design (CAD) in the architecture and engineering professions. The architect or engineer is still crucial to the design process, both in developing the concepts, resolving the ambiguities that inevitably arise as a project unfolds, and interacting with their client to ensure that the design conforms to their needs. Beyond that, the bulk of the detailed work is done by the CAD algorithms. The value generated by these algorithms forms a very significant share of the value delivered to the client. It therefore makes no sense at all to measure that value, or bill the client, in increments of human effort. How much time the architect or engineer spends working on a design remains important, but it is just one facet of how the business measures that professional's performance (in other words, the value that s/he delivers.)

In Type 2, the value is delivered primarily by technology, but that technology is operated by humans. The machine-learning algorithms in use today arguably fall into this category, as do many of the subscription services that law firms operate, which require frequent updating. The professionals operating the technology may be lawyers, or paralegals, but just as easily legal technologists or data scientists. Because the bulk of the value is delivered by the technology, and the cost of the operators relative to the value being produced is relatively low, it makes even less sense for the work to be valued (or billed) in increments of human effort.

Type 1 describes where the work product is delivered entirely by the algorithm, with human input limited to initial design and development, upgrades, and maintenance. Online legal service providers such as those operated by companies such as "LegalZoom" operate within this modality, or at least at the intersection between Types 1 and 2.

Clearly, very different approaches to business model are required to extract the most value from each of the above types of work stream, for the client and also for the law firm.

A great deal of current discussion revolves around the likelihood of legal work moving from Type 4 to Types 2 and 1. In other words, the notion of technology "replacing" lawyers. This is an area where careful thought is required in order to separate reality from hype. As mentioned previously, Frey and Osborne's research indicates lawyers to be in the class of professionals least likely to be replaced by robotics of AI. There is no doubt that many of the tasks previously performed by lawyers (like sifting through millions of pages of documents) is better done by technology. As more data and better algorithms become available, so the range of these tasks will no doubt expand. AI is set to move from mere "machine-learning" to "deep-learning" algorithms. The latter is effectively a subset of the former, the differences being:

- Machine learning uses algorithms to parse data, learn from that and make decisions based upon that learning; and
- Deep learning structures algorithms in layers to create an "artificial neural network" that learns, makes intelligent decisions, and even corrects errors, on its own.

## The limits of deep learning / AI

A great deal of disagreement exists between experts about the limits of what deep-learning might be able to achieve within a reasonable strategic horizon (say, three to five years). It is facile to suggest that deep-learning

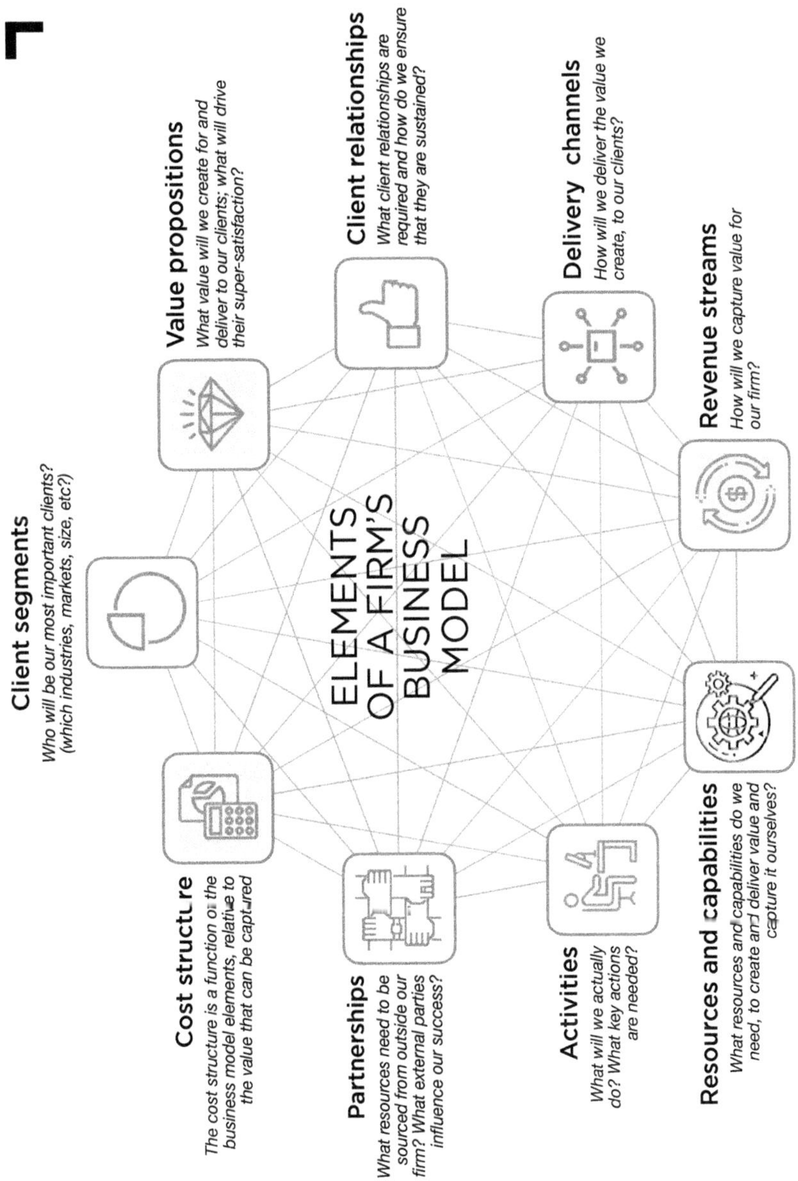


*Figure 2: The elements of a business's business model (adapted from Osterwalder & Pigneur, 2010).*[7]

is without demonstrable limits and, if simply given more time and data, it would easily evolve into the general intelligence suggested by Andrew Ng's 2016 comment that AI would either "now or in the near future" be able to do "any mental task" a person could do "with less than one second of thought".[5] In making sense of today's "volatile, uncertain, complex and ambiguous" (VUCA) world, humans draw on a wealth of tacit knowledge about emotion, human behavior, and culture, to say nothing of the ambiguities of business and society, in ways that are virtually impossible to encode.

This is why MIT Professor Max Tegmark, in his excellent book *Life 3.0: Being Human in the Age of Artificial Intelligence*[6] writes that such general intelligence is at least decades away, which is just as well because it may take that long to prepare society for it. Considerable ethical concerns exist, not only in law but also in medicine and other areas where such AI could have profound impacts on humans and society, about abdicating important areas of authority to machines.

Decades is not an appropriate timeframe over which to consider a law firm's business model and, fortunately, breakthroughs in areas such as deep-learning usually occur in other industry sectors (especially IT itself). Long lead times exist during which lawyers will likely encounter such technologies first in their clients' organization, well before they become serious candidates for "LegalTech" applications.

In practical terms, the above suggests that, in the short-term, law firms need to focus on changing mindsets and behaviors to create a culture that is generally more receptive and welcoming to technology, including in the practice. Doing this requires more than simply investing in the latest machine-learning algorithm or acquiring other apps to support simple processes such as contract review, conveyancing, due diligence, or discovery. This, together with using technology tools such as mobile devices and collaboration platforms more effectively, is probably the start line.

## Digital business transformation, in practical terms

It makes no sense for any business to retool its conceptions of value and its business model without close reference to its customers/clients. As previously outlined, the process should be undertaken in close collaboration with them. Mapping an existing business model is a very different thing to designing a new one and, in an environment where a monolithic model such as the ToL has dominated for so long, simple inertia can be a powerful drag. It is too easy to revert to old, familiar ideas than to grasp new creative ideas, unless clients are present to give input into what they wish to see. The approach of creating an ecosystem of business models around specific solutions, service lines and tasks (instead of retooling the entire firm) makes it easier to make progress and reduces the risk.

Figure 2 demonstrates the complexity of the elements of a business model. Because all nine elements are interconnected, it makes no sense to try to consider one in isolation of the others – certainly not in any comprehensive way. In practical terms, though, one can manage this complexity by approaching it at a local level. Conflating a process to collaborate with a key client to dissect the abovementioned "expectation gap" and so uncover a real issue where it might be bridged, with a process of exploring ways to evolve the business model, is a good way to limit the scope to something manageable, where the likelihood of positive results are greater. Indeed, it may be the only way that ensures that the results of the process are accepted by the firm's partners, and translated into action.

## In summary

In summary, we should be thinking not about how the monolithic ToL business model needs to be replaced in the short-term, but instead about which parts of the business genuinely require a human-leveraged model. We should also be thinking about how that model needs to be modified in order to properly account for the value being created and delivered to clients by the digital tools that firms are building in to their service delivery processes and other "value chains". These tools are increasingly becoming areas of investment. If it has not already arrived, then the time is not far away where it will make no sense to just pass the cost of these tools on to the client as a disbursement, ancillary to the human effort, except in the Type 4 work described in Figure 2.

The work that a firm does for its client needs to be disaggregated over time into units with similar performance drivers, and business models for each type developed so that the correct balance can be struck between the value delivered to clients, and the value captured by the firm, for its partners. The age of a single monolithic business model for law firms is past.

None of the above can be achieved without close consultation and collaboration with those who purchase the services that the law firms sell.

*Acknowledgement:*

Rob Dinning's and Vicky Lockie's contributions to the thinking around the "GC expectation gap" is gratefully acknowledged. Rob is director of legal function co-sourcing at EY Riverview Law and was previously general counsel, operations and technology at Barclays. Vicky was previously GC of Pearson plc and is now an independent consultant to in-house legal teams and law firms.

### *References*

1. Galanter, M. and Palay, T., 1991. *Tournament of lawyers: The transformation of the big law firm*. University of Chicago Press.
2. Christensen, Clayton M. 1997. *The Innovator's Dilemma: When New Technologies Cause Great Firms to Fail*. Boston, MA: Harvard Business School Press.
3. Agrawal, Ajay, Gans, Joshua and Goldfarb, Avi. 2018. *Prediction machines: The simple economics of artificial intelligence*. Harvard Business School Press.
4. Frey, Carl Benedikt and Osborne, Michael. 2013. *The future of employment: How susceptible are jobs to computerisation?* Oxford Martin School, University of Oxford.
5. Ng, Andrew. 2016. What artificial intelligence can and can't do right now. *Harvard Business Review*, 09 November 2016. Accessed on 12 December 2018 at https://hbr.org/2016/11/what-artificial-intelligence-can-and-cant-do-right-now
6. Tegmark, Max. 2017. *Life 3.0: Being human in the age of artificial intelligence*. Knopf.
7. Osterwalder, Alexander and Pigneur, Yves. 2010. *Business model generation*. Wiley.

## Chapter 8:
# Blue Ocean business models in law

*By Jason Moyse, LawMade*

Ask those in the know, and many will tell you that the greatest surfer in the world is Laird Hamilton. However, he's never won a world title in competitive surfing. He doesn't compete. In fact, it's Kelly Slater who holds 11 world titles and has won in excess of $4m in prize money.

Does that mean Laird isn't really worthy of mention as a surfer?

No one would dispute that Laird is an amazing innovator and waterman, who has elevated the sports of surfing, rowing, kayaking, diving, fishing and other domains. He's also invented, mastered or put new twists on activities including windsurfing, kite boarding, water-skiing, and is seen as the primary force behind the stand-up paddle board movement. As a big wave surfer, he pioneered the use of jet ski launches and what is known as "foil boarding". He is also known for curating intense high-performance training and nutrition programs. And like any CEO, he's a pro at evaluating risk and dedicating himself to push through uncomfortable barriers.

If we only looked at competitive surfing as the measure, Laird would not register. This is what makes him a stand-alone category. By the way, he has made a fabulous life financially, both in and out of the ocean.

In management speak, Laird would be delighted to be described as a Blue Ocean – a concept made popular by INSEAD professors and their compelling book.[1] A Blue Ocean strategy captures new demand with a superior product that makes the competition irrelevant. Red Ocean industries are bloody from battle among numerous commoditized competitors. When you think of Cirque de Soleil, it's a unique category and never competed head-to-head with Ringling Brothers, but it certainly made them irrelevant as evidenced by the close of operations after 146 years in business.

So, what does this have to do with legal services?

A new category is emerging, which could be viewed as Blue Ocean. Whilst traditional law firms battle directly, a "law company" offers a broader set of unique services under a different model. Certainly, the Big Four "accounting" firms are increasingly seen as law companies – but they are transitioning legacy organizations rather than building from scratch.

A law company definition is still coming into form, but broadly speaking includes some of the following traits:

- Corporate ownership structure in addition to or in place of a partnership;
- Lawyers are included, but not paramount in delivering services;
- Allied professionals may be equally or more valuable;
- Process excellence and technology are key planks;
- Tasks are assigned to the right resource;
- Tight alignment to the financial and enterprise goals of the client; and
- Supply chain or "ecosystem" mentality and expertise.

Setting discussion aside on the Big Four, this chapter will outline and assess the recent history, current state, and intriguing future of a select few of the more visible law companies, including the now defunct but pioneering Clearspire, Atrium LLT and Elevate Services.

Clearspire offers many lessons for observers and action-oriented entrepreneurs. It's a gift when entrepreneurs are candid about both their success and failure, and co-founder Mark Cohen has bestowed an excellent e-book "The Clearspire Story,"[2] which provides an inside account.

While founded in 2008, Clearspire did not hit the market more fully until 2011 and was a highly visible and unfolding experiment. In Mark's own words, the model was a laboratory comprised of two organizations: an LLC law firm and a services company. The corporate organization housed all of the technological developments and "business of law" elements, whereas the LLC ensured compliance with US regulatory requirements for the "practice of law".

Clearspire invested heavily in its proprietary technology (Coral) and was process-driven in an effort to pare down real estate and other costs, and enable integration between its workforce and global client roster. The technology enabled lawyers (in-house and outside counsel) to work seamlessly and collaboratively across the globe, linking them as never before with business customers. Customers could track matter progress and budget to actuals in real time, as well as access and reuse intellectual work product. The comprehensive platform included multiple systems in a bricolage of document management, records, conflicts, finance, and unified messaging.

Additionally, a middle layer pulled data from the other areas allowing dynamic data flow and information systems for HR, project management and matter reporting. Tying it all together was the user interface serving as both an intranet and extranet.

All of this was in an era when nothing similar existed, especially in one package. Even in 2018, it is still rare to see client-facing collaboration platforms with real-time updates of matter status and work-in-progress billing.

The financial costs for launching Clearspire were startling at the time, given the ambitiousness and highly speculative approach of "build it, and they will come". The initial investment of $5m represented a sunk cost before day one of revenue. Technology was but one piece and the greater significance of Clearspire was the strategic decision to offer fixed fee services in an era when it was still not *en vogue* among the intended client profile of F1,000 companies.

By 2014, Clearspire had ceased operations. So why didn't it flourish, and what lessons have been observed for the benefit of successor law companies? Pundits are keen to query whether Clearspire was simply ahead of its time and the hypothesis now being tested is whether today's market is more amenable.

A successful Blue Ocean business can arise from the most unlikely of conditions. Consider how nascent the video game industry was just a short while ago versus today where budgets exceed Hollywood productions. The flourishing video game studio system is just one part of the ecosystem, and other very unique and successful businesses have emerged. If you haven't heard of Twitch, then you likely don't play and certainly don't watch video games.

Twitch is a video platform focused mostly on video streaming, "eSports" and other live and on demand content. Founded in 2007, Twitch was acquired by Amazon for $970m in 2014. As of 2018, Twitch hosts 2.2 million broadcasters monthly and has 15 million daily active users. The predecessor company was called justin.tv after the founder, Justin Kan.

Through his entrepreneurial journey, Justin consumed a number of legal services ranging from corporate transactional support to litigation defense matters, as well as M&A and everything in between. As both a participant and angel investor through YCombinator, Justin also became familiar with the challenges of technology adoption by law firms, no matter how compelling the efficiency gain or value proposition.

Justin now has his eyes set on legal and is applying Silicon Valley, Lean Startup and YCombinator approaches through Atrium, the law company he founded in late 2017. Atrium shares striking similarities with Clearspire but there are also some key nuances. In terms of the "market" being served, Clearspire pursued well established corporates, whereas Atrium is starting with what Justin knows best: start-ups and emerging high growth companies.

In the last 18 months, Atrium has raised an eye-popping $75m and is comprised of two organizations, one of which is a technology corporation that can receive outside investment of capital. The technology company is designed to be in the service of the sister law firm of 35 full-time lawyers, which complies with the requisite regulations for provision of legal advice. Clearspire and Atrium are similar in respect of their underlying structure and goal to be the consumer of their own innovations, which in turn vastly improves the client experience. Contrast this with the traditional law firm model, which typically attempts to innovate based upon screaming client demand and rarely as a proactive and anticipatory strategy.

Elevate Services is also a law company with a founding team that has decades of experience building legal services business that blend people, process, and technology. While operations commenced a few years ago and they've employed lawyers from the outset, they've recently aligned with US-based Valorem Law Group to create ElevateNext, which performs all "attorney-required" work for clients, while the "attorney-not-required" work is provided by the primary Elevate business. It would not surprise if they continue to grow by acquiring law firms in the UK or Australian markets as permitted through Alternative Business Structure regulations that are not available in the US. Of course, the technology being developed by Elevate is for global client use among law firms and corporates, which is a nuance from Clearspire and Atrium.

The emphasis of law companies for upfront transparency on pricing creates pressures for efficiency at the outset of a matter to be able to deliver and maintain profitability. In the absence of a change order, once the work is scoped, the revenue is baked, and everything must be delivered under those constraints. While law firms have increasingly adopted fixed fee options as well, law companies are uniquely situated to predominantly utilize this measure.

In the case of Atrium, why would it tread where Clearspire struggled, and how might it flourish?

Significant investments of time, resources, and energy on what is essentially a product that doesn't see real combat as quickly as possible is an anathema to the start-up ethos of getting a Minimal Viable Product (MVP) into market. Any new business is really just a testable hypothesis. The first patrons of Atrium were likely willing to sign up and "take a risk" on a provider that has the same approach to building their business as the customers themselves. Atrium definitely speaks the same language as its core start-up customers – which is markedly different to established corporates.

Purchasers buy on emotion and then justify with intellect. Atrium and other law companies like Elevate Services had clients willing to buy before they had services to deliver. Atrium is already climbing the league tables among law providers regarding equity financings with notable Series A to C rounds and approximately 280 customers. That is impressive for a company/firm that only opened their doors less than two years ago, and the decision to use Atrium is influenced by the brand and prior history of the founder(s) in addition to great legal expertise. Elevate's quick rise is also attributable to the goodwill and prior dealings of the founding team and their impressive track records.

When business models, products, services and start-ups fail, it is usually because they spent more time building in isolation then they did testing with (paying) customers. When customers are indifferent, a business is dead in the water. In the case of Clearspire, there was too much building in isolation at significant cost as measured by financial, labor and time spent before launch. Rather distressingly, the stated and articulated enthusiasm of prospective general counsel purchasers did not translate into executing a buy decision. They *loved* the idea intellectually, but would not take any risk for certain types of work to be provided by someone other than the most reputable and venerable of legal brands. No one gets fired for hiring (insert known large firm brand here).

One of the more fundamental differences in approach by Atrium to Clearspire is the application of Lean Start-up methodology and YCombinator staples of Build, Measure, Learn (BLM) as a constantly rotating and iterating process cycle of product and organizational development. The BLM cycle provides constant testing in a live environment with real clients providing feedback to optimize the offering so that it lands, ultimately, with what customers will accept and buy. The faster and more frequent the cycle spins, the more learning leading to adaptations takes place through feedback and observation on defects, gaps, and omissions. You also see what's working and can double down on delight for items that are hitting the mark.

Atrium has also been very selective in the initial types of work it delivers with focus on financings and more recently commercial contracts and blockchain counsel. Many high-end law firms have tailored programs centered squarely towards emerging companies on the front end of their incorporating and early funding process. The firm's hope is for lifetime value clients via supply of upstream legal services upon maturation of the company. That, however, is anything but a sure bet. Many of the firms that agree to take on risk in the early days of a company find themselves disappointed when the juicier (interesting and profitable) work migrates to others. It remains to be seen if climbing the "value chain" is something that Atrium can (or should aim to) achieve.

## Technology – a puzzle piece, but not the panacea

The point of technology for both Atrium and Clearspire is first and foremost to provide quality of life improvements for the legal team members. Often, that equates to just buying the best off-the-shelf technology that's already in existence, but could also mean internal development of proprietary tools. This is an advantage of most law companies, including Elevate, which continues to buy and build as part of its development.

The data that's laden in corporate documents could be purposefully fluid and dynamic, but most importantly, useful. Enormously valuable data is trapped in PDFs, Google Drives, email and of course legal documents like S.E.C. and other regulatory filings as well as contracts. The ability to mine that corpus is, in fact, much easier said than done – but the rewards are worth it. The goal of Atrium is to be a data-driven law firm through a structured platform that leverages originating corporate organizational documents and contract. It would indeed be a technical win to be able to convert narrative text to data, giving it structure, which can then be used in a myriad of ways.

While the early outputs might not seem revolutionary, like automation of cap tables by extracting data from static documents and creating a database, it is actually a step function forward from the traditional environment of mind-numbing Excel spreadsheets. Once narrative text becomes true data, the use cases are tempered only by the imagination. Where there is data, there is insight, and potential fodder for other types of product and fluid workflow creation.

Most of what Atrium is producing from a technology perspective is unseen by the client and is focused on better uses of the inputs toward legal service delivery. While tech enthusiasts pine away for singularity approaching "computational" law with advice rendered completely through some flavour of Artificial Intelligence (AI), it's a lot to ask of business clients to rely exclusively on programmatically or algorithmic delivered outputs. Law companies, for all their innovations, are more often focused on mundane efficiency gains than reliance on machine-produced legal advice. That will shift as technologies improve, but humans are always in the mix.

Augmented rather than exclusive reliance on AI will be the peak use case for quite some time. This still requires an enormous amount of trust to be exchanged from the client to the provider and that will always mean *personal* relationships where large sums of money hang in the balance.

From inception, Elevate has emphasized data science, machine learning and AI, *plus* human intelligence blended together as a key strategic plank of its ongoing development of products and services. Its program is titled E=ME^2 (pronounced "me squared"), or "Elevate uses Machines and Expertise in Everything". Recent acquisitions include LexPredict, led by Dan Katz of Chicago Kent Law School, specializing in analytics, data science training, strategy, and risk management consulting in legal services. LexPredict products (LexNLP, LexSemble, and ContraxSuite) will eventually blend into Elevate's "Cael" Enterprise Legal Management apps servicing corporates and professional firms. The prevailing outputs will include items like "AI data science meets teams of sophisticated human reviewers".

Some of the early projects provide M&A due diligence of contracts for forward clients like Cisco – a shared engagement prior to the acquisition. Additionally, services will include AI-enabled contracts repository management, abstraction and search in CLM (contract lifecycle management), as well as process intake, assessment, process, and workflow. With increasing regulatory complexity related to LIBOR, GDPR, and Brexit, for example, there will be greater need for ingesting and parsing of regulations and rules, then applying them across many jurisdictions worldwide. Other law company outputs include outside counsel guideline compliance and predictive modeling for litigation.

With the ability to start with a fresh canvas, adoption of technology for superiorly efficient and effective workflows is not a challenge for law companies. There is no cultural drag requiring coalitions of merely the willing to effect change. Lawyers at AM100 firms, for example, might go along with new programs of delivering work. They might even readily align with transformational technology adoption in conducting their practice. Then again, they might not. Either way, they will continue to work for the firm without reprimand for not "complying" with the firm's approach, especially in robust practice areas.

Law firm innovation efforts will always have fragmented uptake – even among the most successful – whereas law companies can have a golden thread laced through the entire operation. At law companies, recruited lawyers and allied professionals must contribute more than mastery of substantive legal knowledge via the "practice of law". There is, instead, a law company way to delivery, which you either agree to up front – or elect not to join. Established law firms have consensus-building requirements that take considerable time to navigate and aren't always productive.

### Value creation as a capital idea

Law companies also have much more opportunity to build their businesses without taking money from institutional investors. The approach of Elevate has been to fund its organic growth from equity from its founders and utilize a credit facility from Morgan Stanley to part-finance its acquisitions rather than take equity from a control venture or private equity investor, but as it grows, perhaps that will change.

Additionally, law companies can *create* value in more ways than the incumbents, especially where they develop their own technologies which could either be marketed, sold, licensed, or otherwise extracted for value to an even bigger audience beyond the mothership. A typical law firm that purchases a matter management system would not then turn around and sublease or otherwise convey to someone else. Law companies will be able to service themselves as well as others with developed technology and have revenue lines and intrinsic value of the underlying intellectual property.

There is also a valuation component for a law company that is real and relatively liquid either by further equity investment or straight up acquisition into another business. In many respects, that's what has unfolded among some of the Big Four accounting firms that have acquired technology and services companies, such as Ernst and Young purchasing Riverview Law to support a broad-based multidisciplinary globally diverse operation.

It's difficult to imagine a traditional large law firm having as great an opportunity for other forms of value capture and especially sale as a going concern. In North America, the prospect of a publicly traded law firm is remote. The prevailing regulatory regime postulates that lawyers have a hierarchy of duties to the court and client such that adding a duty to shareholders for asset appreciation and dividends could be viewed as objectionable. In jurisdictions with Alternative Business Structures, this is much less of a concern. For a law company, where lawyers are not the stars of the delivery model, the non-law firm organizations could indeed have share capital changing hands in public and private markets. Share appreciation would float further growth of the offerings and underlying company to the benefit of customers. That's a value multiplier exclusive to law companies over incumbents.

The assets beyond real estate for traditional professional services firms continue to be largely driven by fungible talent. Perhaps you really loved working with a specific AM100 firm for your recent acquisition. Was it truly the firm or the specific client team that served you? If that client team moved laterally to another firm, there's a good chance you would go with them. This is the opposite to technology lead offerings where you are unlikely to change providers when you've had a really great experience and are content with price points. There are significant switch costs in changing well-entrenched solutions, especially when technology is coupled with subject matter expertise.

Atrium is perhaps the most well-capitalized upstart, but their use cases are all driven towards automation, workflow, seamless operations, and essentially getting the legal work delivered without all of the friction that currently drags on law firms with a lack of dynamic data flow. When posed with questions related to computational law, meaning the idea that something like AI could deliver contextually relevant legal service provision in the form of advice without human intervention, there are no such moon shots being aspired to *per se* on the technology side for Atrium.

In short, they're just trying to net out the fundamentals without the encumbrances of organizational and cultural drag preventing adoption and best use of available technology. Lawyers are definitely needed for legal advice, but the support mechanisms should not include armies of assistants who are simply doing tedium-based tasks to produce output.

## How is success measured?

The challenge with new categories of businesses, especially those that take on significant outside capital, is determining what are the proper key performance indicators, both leading and lagging, of which a board should require full account from the CEO. Established Software as a Service (SaaS) metrics include churn rate, monthly recurring revenue, committed monthly recurring revenue, customer acquisition cost, and inbound qualified lead velocity. Law companies have some elements of SaaS, but also deliver hybrid professional services via talented subject matter experts. With a new category of business, it can be difficult to tell what the best measure of success should be in the early days, but client satisfaction needs to be captured, quantified, and acted upon.

Certainly, internal operations can continue to iterate upon efficiency gains, whether that be turnaround time, or transactional cost to produce legal outputs with fewer costly inputs of which traditionally, labor is far and away the greatest expense.

Atrium's investors are world-beating, industry-making, pioneering innovators such that it's worth querying, over and above their belief in Justin based upon his tremendous track record, what are they seeing as the business opportunity at law companies that would cause them to invest such significant sums? After all, this is only the beginning and more capital will definitely follow.

The two main Atrium investors are General Catalyst (GC) and Andreessen Horowitz – a pair of the most globally recognized venture capital firms. Marc Andreessen in particular coined the phrase that "software is eating the world", and from his early days inventing the web browser, has since meaningfully participated in revolution across industries.

GC has a theory that verticalization of full stack businesses is happening across multiple industries and segments, such as, for example, housing. Software is eating the world, but the way to get software into these industries is not with entrenched incumbents who are resistant and not always incented toward adoption. It is better to reimagine and build a business from scratch with technology as part of the core at inception rather than as a bolt on much later in the tenure of the company.

For Andreesen, a mentee of Michael Ovitz, the appeal of Atrium specifically, but legal more broadly, is that there is opportunity to follow something akin to the Creative Artists Agency (CAA) model which proved to be Blue Ocean. Prior to CAA, talent agencies were essentially order takers lacking vision and team strategies in support of their clients. CAA offered specialists who could handle more than just representation for movie and TV roles, but also product endorsements, publishing etc., and could package clients together, including actors, writers, directors – all on the same project – rather than wait for the studio to offer those roles piecemeal. That sounds like the approach of Elevate's ME Squared and full stack mentality of Justin's prior and existing businesses.

### Evolution: not revolution

While Blue Ocean entities, don't look for law companies to be akin to AirBnB or Uber, flaunting their "disruption" muscle and braying at regulators to vault past rules and regulations – even if those regulations were set out from another era to govern a different type of ecosystem. The larger mature state players like LegalZoom have taken on regulators, sometimes with amazing bravado, such as litigating against the North Carolina Bar for restraint of trade. While it is conceivable that law companies would take an aggressive posture and it would make intriguing drama for industry pundits, it is has never been the intention.

The founders of Atrium, Elevate, and Clearspire have little to no interest in bombastically challenging what remain fundamental ethical tenets unique to legal. No one disputes the reasoning behind regulatory ethics in the first instance. However, one can't help but query whether regulations can really meet that standard in the modern era as relates to both business models and technological developments that are much more sophisticated than can be reasonably comprehended by the individuals and organizations charged with governance over the "profession of law' or "business of law".

It is still early sunrise on this aspect of the legal services industry and it would be folly to suggest that law companies will necessarily prevail over traditional players who are not standing still. Law firms have proved resistant for centuries and may always be relevant even if the exact context changes. However, at no time in history has there been as much opportunity for other players to enter the scene and a Blue Ocean wave could easily form to crest. Truthfully, it is more likely for law firms to start to resemble law companies than the reverse. No matter where you launch, a rising tide lifts all boats and (surf) boards alike.

### *References*

1. Blue Ocean Strategy: www.insead.edu/executive-education/strategy/blue-ocean-strategy
2. The Clearspire Story: https://legalmosaic.com/2017/12/11/the-clearspire-story/

# Chapter 9:
# Adapting business models to ride the millennial wave

*By Rachel Brushfield, EnergiseLegal*

In order to keep pace with the changing workforce demographic, law firms of the future will have to adapt their business models to suit the needs of multiple generations. This chapter explores generational differences and their impact on the employer of the future, including motivations and career drivers.

There are now up to five generations in the workplace for the first time, with the youngest generations the most diverse of any in history. These generations have very different values, motivations, needs and wants, and failure to understand these differences can cost organizations dear. Millennials' views need to be sought as they are tomorrow's managers and leaders and they are collaborative in nature and like to be involved in decision-making. By 2020, millennials will make up 50 percent of the global workforce and by 2025, 75 percent. Law firms need to rethink their traditional hierarchies and practices to attract, engage, and retain millennials. Talent is, after all, the source of a firm's competitive advantage. With the emergence of disruptor firms, a freelance career becoming more accessible, as well as non-legal career options such as legal tech and legal industry disruptors more prevalent, law firms not only need to work hard to retain millennials, they need to attract them in the first place.

Millennial lawyers take a broader view of their careers than previous generations, and may move industries during the course of their careers. A clear progression path is essential to attract and retain millennials. Agile/home working is one way of attracting talent to smaller and regional firms. Millennials blend work and life together and this requires decision-makers to re-think when, where and how work occurs.

## What are the five generations?

A generation is a demographic, psychographic, and attitudinal grouping. Characteristics by their very nature are generalizations, but still provide useful insights to guide decision-making. As you read this chapter, be aware of what generation you are and whether you are typical of your generation. I am generation X by birth year, but very much millennial by values, beliefs, motivations, and choices.

### Traditionalists

Traditionalists were born between 1939 and 1947, so are currently aged between 69 and 77. Their planned retirement may have been delayed due to the impact of the credit crunch. They are late adopters of change, need to be in control, and are risk-averse.

### Baby boomers

Baby boomers were born between 1948 and 1963, so are currently aged between 53 and 68. They have invested time and sacrificed work-life balance for increased compensation and status, are reluctant to collaborate, and are focused on earning today rather than planning for tomorrow.

### Generation X

Generation X were born between 1964 and 1978, so are currently aged between 38 and 52. They are independent by nature, demotivated by lack of reward and recognition for time and effort invested, and will move for new opportunities where they feel more valued.

### Generation Y

Generation Y were born between 1979 and 1999 and are aged between 17 and 37. Generation Y are also known as Millennials. They seek feedback and validation, and enjoy working collaboratively. They work to live rather than live to work, and seek varied and fulfilling work with meaning – they want to make a difference. Millennials value working with great people, enjoying the time they spend on the job, working flexibly, and developing new skills.

### Generation Z

Generation Z were born after 2000, so are currently aged 16 or under, and are the managers and leaders of the future. They are often grouped with Generation Y.

Generations Y and Z combined are commonly referred to as "digital natives" or the "net generation" – goal-oriented and achievement-oriented, with a preference for active learning and social activities. Social media and a smart phone is part of their world and how they communicate. Texting rather than phoning is their preference in many cases.

This chapter focuses on the Generation Y or Millennial generation and their impact on tomorrow's law firm and legal profession in the coming years. Employers need to rethink how they attract, retain, develop, and motivate the best millennials for the 21st century workplace, and how their business models reflect this.

## Facts about Generation Y/The Millennials generation

Millennials are redefining the employer/employee relationship. Millennials began their working lives during a global recession as the pace of change accelerated and record unemployment occurred. They are a "work hard, play hard" generation. They plan for the long term and want work that builds their long-term employability. It is important for millennials to maintain their standard of living.

They expect to work longer than previous generations; half expect to work over the age of 65, 27 percent over the age of 70 and 12 percent until they die. Millennials think about their careers in "waves", with changing paths, pace, and regular breaks to sustain them for a longer working life and to allow them to reskill. Eighty-four percent foresee significant breaks. Women anticipate breaks for caring for others; to have children, care for older relatives, focus on supporting their partners and volunteering, whereas men anticipate breaks for relaxation, travel, or holidays. Sixty-one percent of women anticipate taking a break for the birth of their children and 33 percent for childcare, compared with 32 percent and 20 percent for men respectively. Dual income households or "breadsharing" is an ongoing trend. This data reflects the differences between men and women – one of the reasons that women lawyers leave private practice, particularly after their second child, is when the compromise between juggling work and home responsibilities and funding childcare becomes too great. Will this change when millennials become decision-makers? Time will tell.

Seventy-five percent of millennials are currently working in full-time jobs and half are open to non-traditional forms of employment in the future.

Fifty percent of millennials would consider leaving their current job due to a lack of appreciation. Employers such as law firms, many of whom haven't made feedback a priority, need to re-think how they provide recognition and feedback from managers and peers.

The five priorities of millennials when looking for a job are:[1]

1. Money: 92 percent;
2. Security: 87 percent;
3. Holidays/time off: 86 percent;
4. Great people: 80 percent; and
5. Flexible working: 79 percent

Ninety-three percent of millennials want lifelong learning and are willing to spend their own time or money on further training. Four out of five say that the opportunity to learn new skills is a top factor when considering a new job. Twenty-two percent intend to take an extended break from work to gain new skills and qualifications.

Millennials are more likely to stay with an employer because of a pay increase or bonus, a new challenge or promotion, better work–life balance, a clear career path and being recognized by managers and colleagues.

Sixty-three percent intend to stay with their current employer for the next two years or longer. When asked about the "right" amount of time to stay in a single role before being promoted or moving to another job, two-thirds said fewer than two years and a quarter said fewer than 12 months.

Training and development is the most highly valued employee benefit. According to a study from PwC, 98 percent believe that working with strong coaches and mentors is an important part of their development.[2]

Corporate social responsibility (CSR) is important to attract them. Eighty-eight percent say that they would choose employers who have strong CSR values, and 86 percent would leave an organization whose values no longer matched their own. For example, an employer's policy on climate change is seen as important by 58 percent – so it's not just working practices but also social objectives that matter.

The desire of millennials to share knowledge has business benefits in sharing best practice and for employee engagement, but also presents significant risk, for example when a candidate is rejected or there are delays in the recruitment process in the "want it now" generation. Similarly, up-to-date technology and using it in an innovative way is essential to attract them to your firm.

## Implications on organizations

The differences between the different generations have many implications on what organizations have traditionally done in terms of structure and hierarchy, career models, management style, performance management, training and development, succession planning and so on. Millennials will vote with their feet if they are not happy and see leaders displaying inappropriate behaviors, or when they feel there is a mismatch in values.

Below are some common scenarios for organizations. Which ones do you most relate to? How are you preparing to tackle them?

- A younger employer wants to work collaboratively and be involved in decision-making, but their manager likes being directive and making the decisions themselves.
- An organization has a large number of senior workers who want to retire following a long working life with grueling hours. The younger workers do not want the responsibility, long working hours, and commitment that being a senior manager entails as they seek a healthy work–life balance, giving the organization succession planning issues and potential lateral hiring costs.
- Millennials want to receive frequent feedback but their Generation X managers are too busy, don't prioritize this task, and as a result millennials leave with multiple consequences on the organization and a damaged employer brand.
- Generation X have made many sacrifices in their personal lives and are resentful of the flexible working that millennials now enjoy. The attitude "Why should they have it so good when I didn't" permeates, covertly making their lives difficult.
- Senior Baby Boomer managers have made good profits from rising house prices so cannot relate to the need for millennials' demands for a good starting salary and fast progression so that they can pay off student debts and have a chance of getting on the first rung of the property ladder.
- Generation X managers want the certainty of knowing they have the right people recruited to complete a two-year program, whilst millennials want to work on it for six months then go travelling, returning to set up their own online business.
- Baby Boomers and Generation X are used to long face-to-face meetings to discuss and make decisions, whereas millennials communicate in a shorter "Magpie" type way.

There is no "right" or "wrong" about the different generations and how they think and behave. They are just different. There are benefits and dangers in each approach. The key is awareness and understanding the differences so that the positives can be harnessed and the pitfalls avoided. In a nutshell, success is no longer an age; it is an attitude and the celebration of individualism is here. Long-established policies and processes need to be re-examined. Big change takes time and effort and busy executives lack head space to think through and plan such huge shifts in how businesses are run. Why not engage millennials in making these changes happen?

## Attracting and engaging millennials

The following section delivers tips and advice as to how to attract and engage millennials into your workforce.

### Collaboration and responsibility

Carve out quality thinking time away from the day-to-day business activities supported by facilitators in a conducive environment to make some good headway in change. Ring-fencing time in this way is invaluable and ensures that changes are discussed and implemented. Without this approach, the implementation of changed policies and processes can be delayed by more than a year. Millennials are motivated by collaboration and hungry to be involved in decision-making at an early point in their career, so the very act of involving them in discussions engages them.

Give millennials the challenge of how to attract, develop, and engage their generation, supported by an action learning set/group coaching. Empowering a group of young lawyers to take responsibility for this motivates them and provides them with a career enhancing experience that they can use to market themselves later in their career. They love access to senior lawyers in the firm, so the opportunity to present their findings to the partnership or executive board is appealing to them. It can be difficult for someone from a Baby Boomer or Generation X generation to relate to the needs, wants, and motivations of millennials because they are very different to their own and at a different career stage, so better to delegate the problem to the very people you want to understand and appeal to. Bird and Bird, winner of a Managing Partners Forum 2018 Best Programme Award for Leadership Development,[3] goes beyond training, with elements such as the establishment and nurturing of role models, and creation of internal networks in the firm.

Create a junior board with specific responsibilities and accountability. Partners in a law firm carry many responsibilities in addition to fee-earning. Defining specific projects that can be delegated to a junior board will not only motivate millennial lawyers; it will help to develop their interpersonal skills, including listening, questioning, and presenting. Millennials or "digital natives" communicate "in the moment" via text and social media, but need to develop good interpersonal skills to handle clients well and manage and supervise other lawyers. Creating a junior board, having constructive discussions, and creating a business case are useful skills to acquire at an early stage in their career.

Create employee propositions for different employee segments. The employee proposition, i.e. what an individual gets from joining the firm, is a marketing principle applied to people. Different people are motivated by different things, so segmenting employees into different groups and defining the employee proposition for each group helps to make internal communication effective and focused and more likely to engage the target audience. One of my career coaching clients, a millennial, resigned and changed law firms because she wanted to write articles and get involved in business development, but her boss, a partner, would not let her.

**Ongoing coaching and performance review**

Train line managers to adopt a coaching style of communication. A coaching style of communication has the premise that everyone has the answers within them, it is just a question of bringing them out. Managers adopting a coaching style of communication, i.e. asking open incisive questions such as "What are the blocks to progress on this case?" listening to the answers and reflecting back what is expressed encourages the junior lawyer to think for themselves and come up with their own answers rather than do what their manager/supervisor thinks is best. The legal market is experiencing more disruption, and fresh thinking is needed. One of my executive coaching clients, a partner in a law firm and practice group head, ignored her junior staff when they came into her office to ask a question, and didn't understand why they felt demotivated.

Make quarterly career conversations separate to performance development reviews and include in line managers' KPIs and rewards. What gets measured gets done and making the success of direct reports a KPI will ensure that it is a priority. In many law firms, an annual appraisal is done as an afterthought and is not made a priority versus fee-earning. Delays to PDRs taking place or being skipped altogether is common. Also, career conversations may not happen in the performance review, either because of a lack of time or because the manager avoids it because they cannot offer a promotion or pay rise. Millennials are hungry for development/career conversations because they take a long-term view of their career and want to develop skills and experiences that give them future options and more career opportunities. A career conversation does not have to be about a pay rise or promotion; it can be about planning a future secondment to broaden experience, job shadowing to deepen their experience of how different departments operate in the firm, or setting up a skill swap such as reverse mentoring with a partner to understand the role of social media in the marketing mix.

Conduct some qualitative market research, such as focus groups and individual in-depth interviews with the different generations, to get under the skin of expressed and hidden fears and concerns. Market research and insights from the horse's mouth are useful to inform change and help decision-makers understand why it is needed, what benefits any changes bring, and the costs and risks of not changing.

Create/build an internal coach resource. Millennials are hungry to develop and learn at an early stage of their career. It can be a challenge for busy fee-earners to allocate time to develop younger lawyers, so developing internal coaches overcomes the problem. The opportunity to be an internal coach as part of their role provides a different career pathway for staff interested in developing people. This can lead to their future appointment as staff partner, or learning and development manager as the firm grows. Learning and development is a very important factor to attract and retain millennials.

### Understanding diversity

Check that your organization's definition of "talent" includes no age bias. Age bias is common, especially in recruitment, but it is often implicit rather than explicit, so not always easy to diagnose. Law firms historically have been very hierarchical in nature, with responsibilities the preserve of senior lawyers, after time served. It is useful to challenge assumptions about why an individual has to be a certain age to be involved in broader decision-making. Millennials value meritocracy. Using the example of Taylor Wessing's award winning Strategic Client Program,[4] which is about understanding the different touchpoints in the client journey, ensuring a millennial contact on the client side would build strong relationships and communication at all levels, strengthening the client relationship.

Include all generations in the organization's talent committee, not just senior managers from one generation. Diversity creates innovation. Having a range of lawyers at different levels, including millennials on the talent committee, helps to avoid "group think" and recruiting in the image of the senior people already in the firm. People relate to people like them, but in a global marketplace, with more women in senior positions and an increasingly diverse workplace, creating a diverse talent pool helps to attract millennials.

Redefine the meaning of diversity, encompassing all generations. True diversity is about individualism and everyone feeling that they can be themselves at work and that they are valued for who they are and their unique approach and talents. Diversity conversations are commonly about men/women, ethnic minorities, LGBT, disabled etc., so creating your firm's own definition not only helps understanding of different points of views from all the generations, it creates an original take on diversity and inclusion.

### Branding

Ensure that a specific individual is given responsibility for the employer brand. An employer brand helps to attract new talent to the firm, saving time and money. Attracting and retaining talent is one of the biggest issues law firms currently face, so making employer brand management a priority in the firm brings many benefits. Employer branding is an overlap between marketing and Human Resources, so choosing someone with the right skillset internally or appointing a consultant externally is wise for this specialist area. Womble Bond Dickinson, joint second place at the Managing Partners Forum 2018 Leadership Development category,[5] uses technology innovatively to elicit and share stories of how participants and firm leaders have grown professionally. This is very appealing to millennials as it uses technology, something that is important to them, and shows where they can be in the future in their careers.

### Developing talent

Develop an alumni pool of talent. In future, employment will be much more fluid than it is currently in law firms and other organizations. Millennials are keen to develop and enjoy varied portfolio careers, travel, and develop their own businesses. Law firms invest a lot of time, energy and money recruiting and developing staff, and so having an alumni pool ensures that there is a process to keep trained and trusted staff who fit the firm's culture in the fold and use them in future in a flexible way, for a short or longer time. This policy can be very useful, for example using the alumni pool for maternity cover, illness cover, and busy times of year in certain practice groups, (for example family law and wills and trusts). It also saves recruitment fees.

Elicit the values and motivations of all employees and ensure that their role is aligned to these. When a person feels that they are getting what is important to them at work, i.e. their values are honored, and they feel motivated, they are engaged and are much more likely to be productive and high-performing. When they feel the opposite, they are more likely to leave or "cruise" at work, not operating at their full potential. Simple changes – such as having a different supervisor, switching practice group or job redesign – can make all the difference and at minimum cost. This exercise takes little time and provides many benefits to the firm and also the individual.

## Self-reflective questions

Ask your partnership these self-reflective questions to begin discussions on what needs to change to make your law firm fit for juggling the needs, wants, values, and priorities of the five different generations in the workforce at one time.

1. How are the changing demographics in our workforce an advantage for our competitive positioning?
2. What is the best way to create understanding of generational differences and how they are useful?
3. What role can portfolio careers play in workforce planning to engage and retain both millennials and pre-retirees?
4. What is the best way for us to give millennials early responsibility balanced with support to mitigate risk?
5. What behaviors, policies and processes do we need to stop?
6. What behaviors, policies and processes do we need to start?
7. What behaviors and habits do we need to see more of?
8. What behaviors and habits do we need to see less of?
9. How does talent management need to evolve for the new world of work?

## Summary

Law firms need to rethink traditional recruitment, development, and reward policies and processes. Employers who want to attract and retain the best of millennial talent need to offer career security, and make feedback and appreciation a regular occurrence, rather than just once a year at the annual performance appraisal. They must focus on career variety and mobility, be flexible in how they engage talent, and provide collaborative working cultures. Engaging in regular career conversations is essential, rather than avoiding them, and being open to alternative ways of working with millennials, rather than necessarily five days a week employment in the office.

Forward-thinking business models will take into account the need to satisfy the desire of millennials for new opportunities without them having to go elsewhere. Internal or external secondments are one way of doing this, as are creating short-term objectives and plans to achieve them, and allowing for breaks for travel or study. A strong employer brand is important, showing examples of millennials who have progressed. Current partners of law firms should not see talented millennials as a threat to their experience and authority, but as an opportunity to update law firm policies and practices and get their help in making this happen. Fulfillment and making a difference needs to be at the heart of the firm's culture, not just solving clients' problems and making money.

### *References*

1. Manpower Group Millennials Careers: 2020 Vision': www.manpowergroup.com/wps/wcm/connect/660ebf65-144c-489e-975c-9f838294c237/MillennialsPaper1_2020Vision_lo.pdf?MOD=AJPERES
2. PwC Managing tomorrow's people. Millennials at work – perspectives from a new generation: www.pwc.de/de/prozessoptimierung/assets/managing_tomorrows_people_millennials_at_work-perspectives_from_a_new_generation.pdf
3. www.twobirds.com/en/news/press-releases/2018/global/bird-and-bird-receives-recognition-in-six-categories-at-the-2018-mpf-awards
4. https://united-kingdom.taylorwessing.com/en/pressrelease/taylor-wessing-wins-best-client-initiative
5. www.womblebonddickinson.com/uk/insights/news/string-award-nominations-womble-bond-dickinson

# Chapter 10:
# Litigation finance – access to capital as a driver of new business models

*By Scott Mozarsky, Vannin Capital*

The legal profession is experiencing rapid and meaningful transformation. Disruption is being driven by technology, data and analytics, globalization, and the evolution of in-house groups. Another factor that is disrupting the market and accelerating the use of new business models and structures by firms and their clients is access to capital. Litigation finance, in particular, is changing the way that law firms and their clients approach both the practice and business of law.

Litigation finance enables law firms and clients to:

- Leverage capital to overcome obstacles to gaining access to justice;
- Reallocate expenses reserved for legal fees on their P&Ls to investments in their products and employees; and
- Drive expansion and growth.

Law firms are also leveraging litigation finance to better differentiate themselves, while in-house clients use it to turn their groups into profit centers and position themselves as strategic assets rather than solely as service groups.

This chapter will focus on the challenges and opportunities that gave rise to litigation finance as well as the impact it is having in making the legal market function in a more efficient and logical manner. It will also focus on key trends and potential ways that the litigation finance market will evolve, moving forward.

### What is litigation finance?

Litigation finance involves third parties funding some part of a dispute between at least two other parties. It can take many different forms, with litigation finance organizations funding claimants or defendants, fees and/or expenses, and potentially other related costs including, among others, operating costs for organizations involved in a dispute. The most common form of litigation finance involves a funder providing non-recourse funding to litigants (usually claimants) in exchange for a percentage of the ultimate judgment or settlement. This arrangement is not considered a loan because if the claimant loses, it does not owe any money to the funder. So, in exchange for giving up its right to a portion of its upside, the client has had all or a portion of its legal fees and other expenses paid, thereby protecting itself from downside risk.

Litigation finance is not a new concept. Financing has been available to parties to disputes for decades. However, the use of litigation funding has gained a significant amount of momentum over the last 15 years, initially in Australia and the UK, driven in part by the more restrictive rules around law firm contingency arrangements in those jurisdictions. Over the last few years it has gained steam in North America. The rapid adoption of litigation funding by law firms and their clients is being driven to a large extent by the high costs associated with engaging in a litigation or arbitration as well as a desire to leverage alternative fee arrangements to drive growth, increase profitability, and differentiate themselves. More specifically, the factors driving the growth of litigation finance are as follows.

### Access to justice

Small organizations with meritorious claims often do not have the resources to litigate against larger organizations. This is referred to by many in the industry as the David and Goliath problem. Having a funder involved enables smaller organizations to pursue claims and hire high-quality law firms that they normally would not be able to afford. It also enables them to avoid legal fee cost pressure that in other circumstances might cause them to settle a dispute at a significantly discounted rate to the equitable amount that they should ultimately receive. To the extent that the other side in the dispute knows a funder is involved, it recognizes that the smaller company has the capital necessary to pursue the dispute through trial and consequently the larger organization is unlikely to pursue a strategy of filing numerous motions and broadening discovery in order to make the smaller organization exhaust all of its capital quickly in paying legal fees.

### Financial engineering

While litigation finance initially gained momentum as the answer to an access to justice problem, the number of large companies leveraging litigation finance is rapidly increasing. This acceleration has been driven by basic accounting and finance principles. Legal fees are considered expenses in a company's P&L, while funds that a company wins in a litigation are treated as one-time below the line assets on the relevant company's financial statements. Consequently, a company's profits are impacted by the legal fees that it pays each year, but very rarely are the company's financial statements impacted by the proceeds relating to a dispute in which it has prevailed. A company's shareholders are unlikely – for valuation purposes – to give it any real credit for winning a dispute. While a company that wins a large case can leverage capital that it has won to address cash flow challenges, return money to its shareholders through a buy-back or dividend, or to fund an acquisition, rarely will the level of cash that a large company wins reach a level that would be material in the context of the overall size of the company. Therefore, companies are willing to give up a portion of their upside in exchange for eliminating the expense associated with paying legal fees.

**In-house groups as strategic assets**

Another reason that litigation finance appeals to in-house counsel is that it enables in-house groups to be a more strategic partner to the business. Organizations leveraging litigation financing are able to improve cash flows and P&L performance to turn their legal groups from cost centers to profit centers and to enable their companies to save money on legal fees that they can then use to invest in talent, product, or to increase profitability. By identifying opportunities for companies to do so, in-house counsel add value as strategic members of an organization's leadership team that goes beyond providing day-to-day legal advice.

**Law firm growth and cash flow needs**

Differentiation is a challenge in an industry that is commoditized due to the existence of a lot of very good lawyers. Law firms need to differentiate themselves in order to win business and grow. Attorneys and firms are leveraging capital from litigation funders as a form of differentiation by adopting innovative fee structures that provide their clients with multiple options. These fee structures sometimes involve firms taking discounts on their fees through a partial contingency arrangement in exchange for a percentage of the client's proceeds from a judgment or settlement. So long as the client wins its dispute, the law firm is likely to realize more from representing the client than it would have if the client had paid the law firm fees under the traditional hourly rate model. Firms are also highlighting access to litigation funding and relationships with funders in their business development efforts in order to remove obstacles for clients to pursue meritorious claims. As part of this process, firms sometimes leverage the funders' depth of experience in certain subject matter areas as a value add.

**Attractive asset class**

A large part of the finance market is participating in one way or another in litigation finance including hedge funds, investment banks, private equity funds, university endowments, pension funds, family offices, and wealthy individuals. As an asset class, litigation finance has outperformed most others over the past few years. This in and of itself would drive a significant amount of interest from the financial community. However, interest is also being driven by two other factors:

1. The asset class is uncorrelated to the economy and capital markets. As we've learned through the various ups and downs of the global economy over the last few decades, there are always legal claims and disputes regardless of whether the economy is doing well or poorly, and the results of these disputes are not in any way related to how well the economy is performing. In fact, it is possible that litigation finance will gain even more momentum in a bad economy as organizations have less capital to dedicate to pursuing cases with merit and are pressured on costs and expenses, thereby wanting to shift these expenses to a funder; and

2. Litigation finance generally provides an attractive investment cycle. When most private equity groups invest in a company, they expect to sell the relevant company and realize strong returns on their investment over a three- to seven-year period with most deals being in the five- to seven-year range. Litigation finance, on the other hand, generally delivers returns in two to three years. There are exceptions to this as the time period can extend as a result of the time it takes to collect a judgment, longer time periods to reach closure on complex matters, particularly in international arbitration, and appeals. However, many disputes settle and on average funders get returns on their investments in disputes within two to three years of making an investment.

## What are the downsides of litigation funding?

Critics raise a number of concerns with respect to litigation finance.

### Increasing the likelihood of frivolous lawsuits

Given that litigation finance removes financial obstacles to bringing a lawsuit, some argue that it increases the likelihood of frivolous lawsuits. While this argument could have merit for the segment of the market relating to funders providing individuals with small amounts of funding to pursue slip and falls and other claims, it is counter-intuitive for the segment of the industry focused on funding organizations involved in large disputes. In these situations, legal fees often exceed $5m and can be significantly larger than that in certain instances. It is highly unlikely that a sophisticated financial organization would agree to fund a frivolous suit given that litigation finance is non-recourse so if a claimant loses, the funder loses their investment and does not receive anything in return. In fact, funders are often more likely to apply stricter scrutiny to analyzing the merits and potential returns of a case than a law firm, since funders approach each case as an investment in which they could lose all the capital they deploy as opposed to a law firm, which, in most instances, gets paid regardless of the results of a litigation or arbitration.

### Extending adjudication

In certain instances, when a claimant has access to funding and is therefore not under pressure to resolve a dispute before it runs out or spends a lot of money, that claimant is less likely to settle, which means longer trial times. On its face, this argument makes sense. That said, this is not necessarily problematic in that one of the benefits of funding is that it relieves pressure on claimants to settle for amounts that are well below the amounts that are more in line with an equitable resolution to the dispute. Also, funding can accelerate resolution of a dispute through settlements by discouraging defendants from leveraging tactics to get the claimants to spend more money such as filing unnecessary motions, which creates delays and unnecessarily extends the litigation process.

### Increasing the number of lawsuits

Common sense is that as parties have access to funding, they are more likely to move forward with claims. While frivolous claims are unlikely to increase, removing financial barriers to bringing a lawsuit very well might increase the overall number of lawsuits filed. Generally, commercial litigation funders do not move forward with the very large majority of cases that they review and the likelihood of litigation funding having a material impact on the large number of cases filed across the US each year is remote. Also, there is a strong argument that an increase in the number of lawsuits, so long as they have merit, is not a bad thing. The purpose of having a justice system is to provide people and organizations who are aggrieved with access to justice and remedies.

### Are there any legal or ethical concerns regarding litigation funding?

As the litigation finance industry has grown, it has gained acceptance in courts across the US and Canada. For example, in a 2013 decision in *Lawsuit Funding LLC v. Lessoff*, New York Supreme Court Justice Bransten noted that, "There is a proliferation of alternative litigation financing in the United States, partly due to the recognition that litigation funding allows lawsuits to be decided on their merits, and not based on which party has deeper pockets or stronger appetite for protracted litigation".

Similarly, in *Hamilton Capital VII, LLC, I v. Khorrami, LLP*, the court held that "...modern litigation is expensive, and deep pocketed wrongdoers can deter lawsuits from being filed if a plaintiff has no means of financing her or his case".

US courts have also consistently held that usury laws do not apply to litigation funding because non-recourse arrangements are not loans. Similarly, the concepts of maintenance and champerty have not been an obstacle to litigation funding in the US, given safe harbors that exist for significant investments involving sophisticated parties. The ongoing debate pertaining to litigation funding is currently primarily focused on a few issues, discussed below.

#### Attorney–client privilege and work product

Given the level of analysis required for a funder to analyze a potential large investment in a dispute, it is fairly common for the funder to be able to review attorney work product and other documents. Claimants, their counsel, and the funder obviously do not want sharing these documents to breach confidentiality and make the documents discoverable. US courts have found that the attorney–client privilege and work product protection are applicable to certain disclosures made to the litigation funder. For example, in *Devon IT, Inc. v. IBM Corp.*, No. 10-2899, 2012 U.S. Dist. LEXIS 166749 (E.D. Pa. Sep. 27, 2012) the court held that that documents shared between a party and litigation funder under confidentiality, common interest, and non-disclosure agreements were privileged under the common interest doctrine. The court indicated that under "these controlled conditions, there was no waiver of" attorney–client privilege.

Similarly, courts have consistently held that a party's communications with actual or prospective funders are shielded from production based on the work product doctrine, which protects "documents and tangible things that are prepared in anticipation of litigation or for trial by or for another party or its representative (including the other party's attorney, consultant, surety, indemnitor, insurer or agent)". (Fed. R. Civ. P. 26(b)(3)(a).) Communications between a party, its attorneys, and litigation funders necessarily contain and reflect "opinions by… counsel regarding the strength of… claims, the existence and merit of… defenses, and other observations and impressions regarding issues that have arisen in this litigation," and fall squarely within this protection. (*Doe v. Society of Missionaries of Sacred Heart* (N.D. Ill. May 1, 2014).)

Courts have also consistently held that "the terms of the final agreement, such as the financing premium or acceptable settlement conditions reflect an analysis of the merits of the case". (*Carlyle Investment Management v. Moonmouth Co.* (Del. Ch. Feb. 24, 2015).) With this in mind, the first thing that reputable litigation funders do when engaging with a potential client is get an NDA executed.

### Duty of loyalty

Attorneys have a duty of loyalty to their clients. This duty requires litigation counsel to act in a client's best interests and give the client independent legal advice without interference from third parties. The duty of loyalty is an important consideration in litigation financing. A funder that controls a litigation creates issues regarding counsel's ethical duties of loyalty and independence. In order to ensure that they do not create problems with respect to the duty of loyalty, third-party funders take steps to ensure that they do not control the litigation. They do not hire or terminate counsel, direct litigation strategy, and/or make settlement decisions.

### Disclosure

There is ongoing debate regarding whether a party being funded by a third party should have to disclose to the other side the terms of the relevant financing arrangement. Those who do not support disclosure argue that disclosing terms of financing arrangements is unfair because the other side will know details regarding the funding that its adversary has available to it, the budget for the relevant dispute, etc. The party receiving this information can then deploy tactics that put pressure on available funding and budget. A middle ground approach would be for the relevant parties to disclose the existence of a funding arrangement and the identity of the funder. To the extent that additional information is required to address concerns about conflict and duty of loyalty, an approach that has been followed by some courts is to have the disclosure made ex parte and in camera to the judge, which means that the judge will know details about the financing, but the counter-party will not. Judges have made clear that the purpose of the disclosure is to affirm that there is no conflict and the funder exercises no control over the matter. In these situations judges have indicated that no discovery will be permitted into the litigation finance arrangements, which they recognize constitute protected attorney work product.

### Law firm/funder agreements

While courts have consistently held that litigation finance arrangements between funders and clients are valid, one area that is strongly debated is direct agreements between law firms and funders. Some argue that in situations in which a funder enters into a non-recourse financing arrangement directly with a law firm, such an arrangement gives non-lawyers a right to the legal fees from particular matters and could create situations in which non-lawyers improperly influence the lawyer's independent judgment. However, the view held by a large majority of the legal community is that it does not make sense that lenders and law firms have been permitted to enter into recourse loan agreements in which law firms agree to covenants permitting banks to influence the firm's operations based on defaults, but may not agree to a non-recourse loan, where the lender has no power over the firm.

### How are litigation finance deals structured?

Litigation funders generally have a significant amount of flexibility in how they structure deals. Unlike law firms, litigation finance organizations can help clients during the time of a dispute by funding other client expenses, such as operating costs. Funders also come into matters at various stages, ranging from the period prior to a claim being filed, all the way through to the judgment stage. Some of the most common forms of litigation finance are listed below.

### Single case funding

The simplest form of litigation funding involves a funder committing to a client that it will fund fees and other expenses for a single case. In this situation, the funder assesses the merits of the case as well as potential damages. Assuming the parties reach an agreement, the funding is provided in accordance with an agreed budget.

### Portfolio funding

Portfolio funding involves a funder committing to fund a group of cases as a portfolio. Returns are paid to the funder from the proceeds of all cases. This enables the funder to diversify its risk and provide more competitive pricing as successful cases can subsidize unsuccessful cases.

### Defense funding

Defense funding can take many different forms. The most straightforward is when there is a dispute over an asset, whether that asset be a company, rights to a revenue stream, etc. In exchange for funding a defendant, the funder's upside if its client prevails would be either a revenue stream over a period of time or equity in the relevant asset. Another form of defense funding involves the parties agreeing on the level of loss that would constitute a "win" and the funded entity making a payment if such a win is achieved. A last form of defense funding involves a funder committing to pay the legal fees for a case in which a company is a defendant as part of a portfolio consisting of other cases in which the relevant company is a claimant.

## What are the trends in litigation finance and how is the industry likely to evolve?

The litigation finance market is growing rapidly. It is still early days in the US, with rates of adoption varying across different geographies, segments, and case types. Given the size of the US market, it will be a number of years before the market reaches a mature state. As the market evolves, portfolio and defense funding are likely to become more prevalent. Funders, law firms, and their clients are also likely to expand the use cases associated with funding – for example, using funding in types of disputes that go beyond litigation and arbitration. Another example is using litigation funding to clear risk in M&A transactions. Technology, data, and analytics will also become a larger part of the funding equation as funders leverage data and analytics regarding cases, law firms, and clients as part of their investment analysis.

# Chapter 11:
# Access to capital – the future of legal markets

*By Jae Um, Six Parsecs*

In the past few years, we have seen unprecedented levels of capital flow into the legal space. The partial views of funding activity we see from various sources imply an already high level of energy as well as money invested into legal innovation. Further, those investments (and one would presume, attendant efforts) only appear to be increasing:

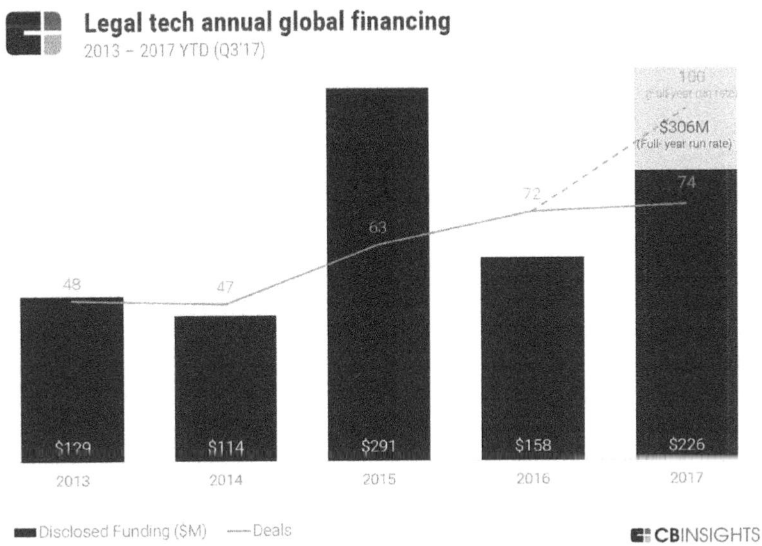


And yet the market appears awash in disillusionment. Many established thought leaders and influencers remain skeptical about the actual impact (or lack thereof) of these developments. Pinpoint signals from corporate buyers indicate a glacial pace and highly uneven distribution for meaningful improvements in service experience and value delivered. And the PeopleLaw sector remains woefully underserved, even as legions of practitioners outside the strongholds of Big Law struggle financially.

## Regulatory constraints affect capital flow (in obvious and non-obvious ways)

Like many other features of the legal industry, the flow of capital investment in this space is littered with idiosyncrasies. The regulatory barriers to non-lawyer ownership have been debated *ad nauseum* elsewhere, but bear mention here. The blindingly obvious implication is that this severely limits the pool of available sources for equity capital into businesses that practice law.

The current regulatory scheme has three less obvious implications on legal innovation as well as the mechanics of how innovation efforts are funded and governed:

### 1. The role of incumbents (law firms and lawyers)

It secures for incumbents (law firms owned and largely operated by lawyers) a material role in deciding when, where, what and how the entire industry will change. This, of course, is a feature, not a bug: protectionism is intended to establish clear and insurmountable advantages for the artisan guild.

It is true that law firms have resisted change and thus bear full responsibility for the current state of the industry. The fact remains, however, that incumbents must be included in any serious dialogue about legal innovation. Regardless of their performance to date, law firms are both financial sponsors of, and direct participants in, legal innovation.

### 2. Practice versus business of law

The requirement of lawyer ownership calcifies unhelpful divisions between the "practice of law" (the domain of lawyers, with limited access to capital) and the "business of law" (a set of enabling activities for legal practice, in the domain of... everyone else with varying non-lawyer titles). These divisions extend deep into our collective consciousness and they do serious harm. not only to workplace cultures, but also the rigor and clarity of our thinking about legal innovation.

This distinction creates an artificially binary model that fails to accurately represent the reality of how legal teams serve clients in the real world. Ultimately, this type of thinking favors incremental improvements to the status quo and R&D based on misguided and antiquated assumptions. It's akin to exploring a closet with the lights off.

### 3. Follow the money

The requirement of lawyer ownership also diverts a great deal of available capital into non-core segments of legal services. This has a dramatic effect on the experience of the end-users and shapes their expectations and appetites. This is, at least in part, why "legal tech" receives a disproportionate share of both capital and attention in the legal innovation dialogue – a lot of money is going into a disproportionately small part of the value chain.

Wiser and more knowledgeable minds continue to discuss the desirability and feasibility of changing the regulatory moat around lawyer ownership. In the meantime, this discussion will remain premised on the status quo, in the spirit of focusing on factors that can be influenced by individual market actors.

## Who funds innovation and why?

Due to the idiosyncrasies of the legal markets, it is helpful to think about innovation in two simple categories: the typical/conventional financial sponsor versus atypical sponsors unique to the legal innovation ecosystem.

The archetype for the traditional financial sponsor of a new venture is the private equity firm. PE firms (inclusive of angels and venture capital shops) are themselves commercial enterprises. Essentially, they offer specialized expertise in the strategic deployment of capital for wealth creation. To put it as simply as possible, PE firms invest capital to buy part or full ownership of companies, apply their expertise to make those companies more valuable, and then sell those companies (hopefully at a higher price point than at purchase).

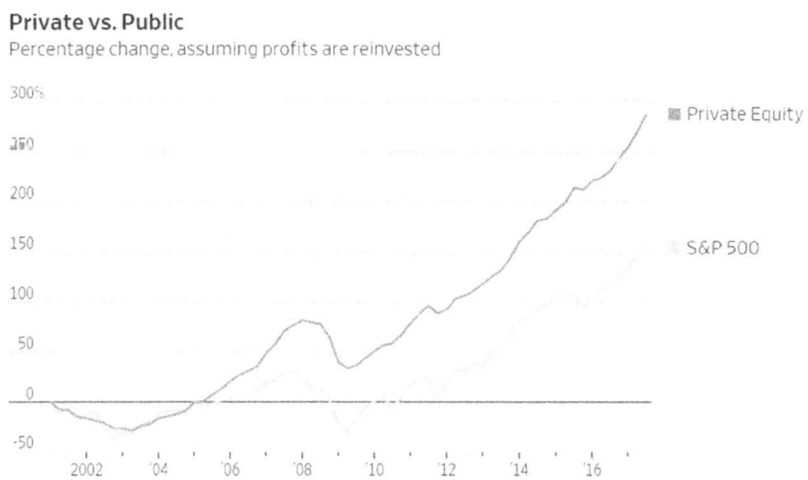


Source: Preqin via *Wall Street Journal*

PE firms attract capital from investors (typically institutional or ultra-high net worth) with investment theses that communicate a unique viewpoint about market opportunities; they retain investors through sustained performance in generating high returns. The below chart is an extremely simplified and theoretical comparison of PE returns against the S&P 500. There are many caveats about the difficulties inherent in comparing apples to oranges but suffice to say that the ROI expectations are high.

Of course, the ultimate returns to investors are abstractions in that they aggregate the outcome of the PE firm's many activities, both successes and failures alike. To put this into more concrete context, it is helpful to think about private equity investments at the company level (again, a simplified, theoretical exercise).

- **Holding times.** On average, PE firms hold portfolio companies for about six-and-a-half years, although early-stage venture capital investments will have longer holding periods (sometimes much longer).
- **Returns/exit multiples.** Target multiples are more difficult to generalize than holding times. Venture capitalist Fred Wilson of Union Squares Ventures is famous for saying often that he looks for one investment that "will return the whole fund." This is a different way of indicating that VCs usually make many high-risk investments with the expectation that most will fail, with a few wins that will make the losses look minuscule. Still, it's probably a safe and meaningful rule of thumb to say early stage VCs will seek something in the neighborhood of 10x returns while mid-stage investors will be looking for a 3x to 5x range.

Funding innovation is both a means to effectuate and a happy by-product of the PE firm's *raison d'être*: generating returns for investors. As we will see, things are not so simple in legal markets.

Simply put, most legal start-ups require a long bake for a relatively small pie. In addition, the vast majority of legal start-ups are point solutions targeting niche markets that are far too small to ever reach the size and scale needed to attract traditional venture capital interest – at least in part due to the highly fragmented composition of the legal services market, as well as the added layer of geographic silos imposed by jurisdictional differences.

The innovation theater that often happens (inadvertently or otherwise) across the law firm landscape is more analogous to the recent explosion in corporate innovation.[1] With technology driving a faster pace of change and start-ups eating into every major sector, mature businesses of all shapes and sizes have embraced the mantra: "what got you here won't get you there". This has fueled mystique around the "intrapreneur", a rash of innovation "labs" housed within staid and stable companies, and the rush to co-opt start-up-style innovation and strategy tools, all with mixed results.

As always, there are lessons to be gained from the mistakes of others, even those outside our own domain. Drawing from the hard-earned lessons of corporate innovation programs outside of legal, two reliable litmus tests emerge to gauge the innovation maturity of established firms:

- **Why?** Clearly articulated **strategic objectives for innovation investments,** tied to financial KPIs that measure the impact on the core business or progress toward profitable exit; and
- **How?** Process and governance around **build, buy or partner decisions.**

## A few bright spots exist

Yes, many law firms engage in some level of innovation pantomime for hype and awards, simply to keep up with the Joneses. But a few law firms do think and act with the recognition that they are future-proofing their businesses against emerging threats. Countless firms are now engaged in serious efforts to integrate process, technology and legal operations to both manage costs and improve service delivery. But a sustained product/solutions focus to spin up new offerings to the market remains more the exception than the rule.

The wide variety of motivations for incumbents to invest in innovation explain, at least in part, why it is difficult to generalize about legal innovation. Some of the variation can be explained by the extreme fragmentation of the marketplace and the resulting dispersion in market position and thus strategic opportunities available to each player. The fact remains, however, that rigorous attempts to measure and compare innovation investments, maturity or performance will need to consider these differences.

## Capital for legal innovation – current state and emerging trends

A survey of the current market landscape, as well as recent developments/dialogue, suggests there are four key trends to watch in the next three- to five-year timeframe.

1. *Liquidity events* suggest sorting/matching behavior by market participants;
2. *Platform + bolt-on strategy* by serial acquirers and mature scale-ups;
3. *Smart money eyeing legal*, to the tune of $500m+; and
4. *Capital gets creative*: working around the regulatory moat.

## 1. Liquidity events – not necessarily a Silicon Valley-style bonanza

2018 has already seen a number of deals that have raised many questions (and inspired many hot takes). The below graphic picks out a small selection of headliners. Given that financial terms are rarely disclosed, the LegalZoom secondary investment attracted a lot of attention by virtue of deal size and resulting valuation.

Liquidity events have a generally pleasing air of a positive development; certainly, they usually involve some people coming into a large lump sum of money. Without raining on anyone's parade, it bears mentioning that the overall texture of recent liquidity events in legal markets indicates that a few different forces may be in play:

- The Avvo, BAL and Riverview Law deals give indications of a strategic sorting in which major players with strategic goals acquire specific assets; in contrast, the Lawyers On Demand and LegalZoom deals feel more like capital churn/injections that will lengthen the runway for these companies to prove out an independent scale/growth strategy that may still be in the works while providing liquidity back to the early stage investors;

- Traditional PE exit strategies favor strategic acquirers and IPOs over financial sponsors, who tend to be more sophisticated and able to negotiate a lower purchase price. Those dynamics may or may not hold in legal markets; the available data is too scant to speculate; and
- The exits by BCLP and DLA Piper raise an interesting question about the optimal role of most law firms in the midwifery and nurturing of new ventures. Law firms have unique assets that make it a fertile environment for experimentation and testing – whether they are well positioned to hold their equity positions to a late exit remains to be seen.

**2. Platform + bolt-on: next-level serial sorting**

The activities of serial acquirers and emerging platforms deserves some mention.

- Unsurprisingly, Thomson Reuters and LexisNexis remain most active acquirers as they supplement internal innovation agendas with strategic M&A. LexisNexis, in particular, has been aggressive in sourcing new product and service innovations through recent acquisitions of Ravel Law, Intelligize, and Lex Machina – all prominently on display at the recent AALL conference. In contrast, Thomson Reuters' recent launch of WestLaw Edge appears to be powered much more heavily by internal innovation and R&D;
- Epiq, Consilio, and Mitratech are all PE-backed and have access to the capital to continue bolt-on deals to round out their market offerings. Most recently, Mitratech acquired ThinkSmart for an undisclosed sum;
- Relativity may emerge as a likely platform looking for bolt-on acquisitions; the company has invested in Heretik and HealthJoy, signaling financial commitment to extend its platform beyond eDiscovery into contracts and highly regulated data stores; and
- Earlier this year, Elevate announced that it had secured a line of credit from Morgan Stanley Expansion Capital to fund its growth. Elevate did disclose that the proceeds would be spread out across strategic acquisitions as well as investments in product and service expansions.

### 3. "Smart Money" from Silicon Valley continues to eye legal vertical

Independent research conducted by Six Parsecs indicates that "Smart Money" VCs (the Silicon Valley elite, as identified by CB Insights) have invested in almost 30 legal tech companies in funding rounds totaling over $500m. This list includes some of the most recognizable names in legal tech, including Avvo, Clio, DocuSign, LegalZoom, and Ravel, as well as some newer names to watch like Atrium LTS, Casetext, Ironclad, Judicata, Modria, and SimpleLegal. Famed Valley seed accelerators Y Combinator and 500 Start-ups have been fairly active as well, funding over 20 start-ups in rounds totaling almost $180m.

An interesting counterpoint to the "Smart Money" portfolio are the investments made by Ulu Ventures. While Ulu's legal start-up portfolio is small, it includes Lex Machina and Ravel Law, both acquired by LexisNexis. Ulu founder Clint Korver was part of an early cohort of VCs who were early adopters and customers of legal start-ups as an alternative to incumbent firms (and expressed intense skepticism about the waves of change washing over Big Law); that cohort included Foundry Group founder and ex-Cooley lawyer Jason Mendelson, whose claim to fame included, among other things, hating on start-up lawyers. This raises some interesting questions about what legal start-ups might need more: capital to fund growth or advisors with a keen understanding of the domain.

### 4. Capital gets creative – workarounds for regulatory barriers

While only orthogonal to this discussion, the emergence and growth of litigation finance must be noted. Litigation finance is a rare bird in legal innovation that fits into Marc Andreessen's "huge, if true" paradigm. According to BTI Consulting, litigation made up nearly 30 percent of the demand for all outside counsel services in 2018; while a rough proxy, the share of litigation spend in all outside counsel budget still gives an idea of the significant addressable market size for litigation finance. Since 2014, litigation funders have raised capital in excess of $3bn.[2] While still in its early days, litigation finance has the potential to reshape the current landscape for a huge segment of the legal services market, and represents a creative channel for outside capital to influence and ramp up investment into legal data handling and predictive analytics.

## Access to capital: could be better, but not the choke point

Research by Six Parsecs suggests that the total amount of hard capital invested into legal tech, legal services and adjacent spaces is in all likelihood much, much larger than the $998m estimate reported by CB

Insights in 2017. Further, is impossible to account for all of the soft investments made by existing players to fund strategic projects, initiatives, feasibility tests, as well as the ongoing payroll of the growing roster of internal innovation teams across the legal space.

The aggregate amount of capital invested in legal isn't the issue – the more serious problem is the inefficiency in finding and funding the right opportunities. However, emerging trends suggest that access to capital is getting and will get more efficient over time.

Upcoming instalments will make the case that inefficient access to markets and talent are much more serious barriers to innovation maturity in legal markets. That said, a rigorous look at capital flows in our industry is still important.

Why? Because there is no better accelerant for #realtalk than the topic of money. Discussion of capital must necessarily address the question of returns. Too often, we across the legal industry use innovation as an emotional lift – workshops and brainstorming sessions usually make us feel better and more hopeful about the future. Where accountability mechanisms are absent, good feelings often provide sufficient returns for these costs.

Looking at the current state of the legal innovation landscape through this unforgiving lens can produce unexpected clarity. For the industry to mature beyond isolated experiments at the edges, we must engage in more rigorous thinking about (i) what innovation experiments actually cost, (ii) what returns they generate, and (iii) how both sides of the equation fare as the endeavor scales. Not all the inputs and outputs of innovation efforts will be quantified in dollars, but much of it can and should be.

The capitalists will enter the US legal mainstream sometime between a few years from now and never. But in the meantime, those on the inside could stand to take a page out of the capitalists' playbook, starting with the notion that investable ideas must focus on value rather than novelty. Not all new things are better than the status quo, and not all old things are bad enough to be discarded; much like handsome and stupid, innovation is as innovation does.

### *References*

1. www.cbinsights.com/research/corporate-innovation-labs/
2. www.law.com/americanlawyer/2018/06/28/litigation-funders-face-their-hardest-sell-big-law/?slreturn=20181103092531

# Chapter 12:
# AIM – how listed law firms may change the future of the UK legal sector

*By Rachel Khiara, Khiara Law*

In this final chapter, we consider the future of the legal services market in the UK as firms dip their toe into the public domain and a new group of "Public Circle" firms emerge alongside the Magic Circle and Silver Circle in the UK market.

## Liberalizing the legal services market

One of the benefits of the liberalization of the legal services market was to allow firms to raise new capital for expansion and investment in infrastructure and IT. Early expectations were a flood of initial public offerings – the legal Big Bang. Partners would sell out; make their fortune. Yet firms were not keen to invite external investment, and investors were not clambering over themselves to enter the legal services market. Surprising, perhaps, given that law firms are profitable businesses and the legal services market generates £30bn in revenues a year.

But here lies the conundrum. A legal services business is an investment in its people. Without the rainmakers and big hitters, the firm's value plummets, making it notoriously difficult to value a law firm. Investors feared a plethora of key man exits and so it was not until five years after the Solicitors Regulation Authority became a licensing authority of alternative business structures under the Legal Services Act 2007 that some more innovative businesses have gone public. The market held their breath as Gateley plc launched, followed by Keystone Law plc, Gordon Dadds plc, and Rosenblatt Group plc. All, at present, have been looked on favorably by investors and share prices have risen. Success for the new "Public Circle".

## The future?

So, given this change, should an IPO be on the partners' agenda of every ambitious mid-tier firm? Before looking at the pros and cons, it is worth considering the traditional model through which law firms operate – the partnership or limited liability partnership. These models are introspect, secretive and governance is, by and large, entirely a matter for the partners. Profit and capital arrangements are flexible and tax effective. Capital paid in is returned to exiting partners, often without return, and no uplift in value to reflect goodwill or increased valuation of the business.

So how would this change? On flotation, partners would be able to crystallize goodwill, freeing up capital tied up in the business, and invest in the growing business subsequently.

An IPO also generates a capital injection for mid-tier firms to boost weak balance sheets, and invest in new technologies, particularly AI products in the conveyancing, probate, and wills sectors, to deliver services to clients efficiently, giving them a competitive advantage, in a market where differentiation is key to success, or perhaps survival. Partners in those firms are typically reticent to make additional capital contributions themselves, particularly where the more senior (and older) partners on whom the burden would fall the greatest, may retire before seeing the benefit of their investment.

However, with its cash benefits, flotation also brings with it scrutiny and accountability. Decisions are no longer taken by the partners, but instead centralized in a board, which owes a primary duty to shareholders.

Shareholders also need a return on their investment. And this is where the appeal of joining the Public Circle falls away for the larger firms, who do not need a working capital injection, and whose profit shares are at a stable and healthy level. Sharing profits, even with the prospect of capital growth, holds less appeal. But for a mid-sized firm, with a weak balance sheet and profit shares vulnerable to success or otherwise annually, and operating in a market where to ensure profitability involves working longer hours, the appeal is somewhat greater.

Investors do recognize, however, that law is, generally speaking, good business and since liberalization of the market we have seen innovative and disruptive business models that are proving attractive to investors – Gateley and Keystone being prime examples. Yet still, the value remains largely with the talent. So for an investor, the key issue is retention of talent, particularly where partners have divested themselves of the management and strategic direction of their firm, and are now accountable to the board of directors, which is concerned primarily with its shareholders.

Many firms will insist on a partner lock-in of at least a year. Investors may sweeten that pill with a guaranteed profit share, which is likely to be well received. It is also likely that the goodwill consideration will vest over a period of time, possibly as long as three years, to bed in and secure a stable and successful business model before the original partners, should they choose, cash out and retire.

The final carrot is the prospect of investment in the plc, through share options, which may be granted at a favorable price at completion of the transaction, exercisable in years to follow. This is also attractive for up and coming associates, many of whom do not in any event want to follow the traditional trainee to partner road.

So the final hurdle is the regulatory framework, which despite IPOs being anticipated, fails to accommodate a plc model. Issues such as client confidentiality may conflict with public duties of disclosure, and treading the fine line between compliance across regulatory regimes is a constant battle for listed firms. In addition, the legislative obligation on the SRA to pre-approve any non-lawyer with an interest greater than 10 percent is often not possible for plcs. The purpose of AIM – the London Stock Exchange's international market for smaller growing companies – is to trade, and therefore shareholdings may constantly be changing. The plc will not be aware of these movements, let alone be able to seek approval for material interests in advance. These and other issues remain barriers to further IPO activity, but at the very least, there are success stories in the UK market, making this an exciting space to watch for anyone involved in running a legal services business anywhere in the world.

www.ingramcontent.com/pod-product-compliance
Ingram Content Group UK Ltd.
Pitfield, Milton Keynes, MK11 3LW, UK
UKHW021848150926
8657IPUK00005B/150